HIDDEN HISTORY *of* CHILTON COUNTY, ALABAMA

HIDDEN HISTORY *of* CHILTON COUNTY, ALABAMA

Billy J. Singleton

Published by The History Press
Charleston, SC
www.historypress.com

Cover images provided courtesy of the Alabama Department of Archives and History and the Chilton County Extension Office.

Images not credited are courtesy of the author.

First published 2022

Manufactured in the United States

ISBN 9781467152174

Library of Congress Control Number: 2022939487

For Sylvia,
my lifelong partner in our journey through the past and into our future.

Contents

Preface

I have a confession. Even though conventional wisdom dictates that living for the moment is the secret to a more fulfilling existence, I prefer to live in the past. I find that I agree with President Harry Truman, who wrote, "The only thing new in this old world is the history we don't know." I also believe that historical facts are far more interesting and compelling than the most creative work of fiction produced by a best-selling author.

I have been accused of passing acquaintances on the street without speaking, seemingly deep in thought, my mind a thousand miles away. I can only apologize and explain that while strolling along the streets of a community, my thoughts are not a thousand miles away but, most often, one hundred years or more in the past. I frequently find myself imagining what it must have been like to stand on a particular street corner observing the daily events of a previous generation.

I believe that every community, building and individual has a story to tell. These stories are unique, often unusual, sometimes tragic, occasionally humorous but always fascinating and entertaining. Even though it can be a difficult and frustrating task to uncover the details that make an individual or place unique, the effort is never disappointing. Because stories, like memories, tend to evolve with the passage of time, it is the duty of the researcher to document the facts of a subject to provide a true and correct history for future generations.

In 1927, the Clanton Study Club produced the first history of Chilton County. Thirteen years later, T.E. Wyatt, editor of the *Union Banner* newspaper, published *Chilton County and Her People*, a wonderful compilation of facts, biographies and descriptions of events that span the history of Chilton County. In 2000, the Chilton County Heritage Book Committee produced *The Heritage of Chilton County*, an extensive project that embodies the people, places and events of more than one hundred years of local history. Complementing these distinguished efforts, individual community, church and school histories provide the researcher with valuable insight into lesser known but equally important aspects of the history of Chilton County. This book, *Hidden History of Chilton County*, would have not been possible without the dedicated efforts of those who came before to establish the foundations of local history.

Many of the stories included in *Hidden History of Chilton County* originally appeared in the *Clanton Advertiser* during my tenure as a community columnist for that publication. As a writer focusing on local history, I had the opportunity to travel throughout Chilton County to investigate a variety of stories relating to the people and places of our past. These travels led me to the musty basement of the Chilton County Courthouse to review old deed books; to snake- and insect-infested marshes adjacent to the Coosa River, following abandoned rail lines; to weekends spent walking among the headstones of cemeteries seeking biographical information on past generations and days spent in the Chilton-Clanton Public Library archives reviewing thousands of pages of books and old newspapers to link together scattered pieces of information to create a more accurate and complete narrative.

Even considering the snakes, poison ivy, briars, heat, eye strain and other afflictions that plague a researcher of local history, I treasure the experiences and the satisfaction of seeking answers to age-old questions that afflict people like me. As poet and philosopher Ralph Waldo Emerson suggests, "It's not the destination, it's the journey." *Hidden History of Chilton County* is the compilation of my personal journey seeking those unique, often unusual, sometimes tragic and occasionally humorous stories that define the history of a county and its people.

It is my hope that these stories will inspire other novice historians to pick up their notebooks and take the first step on a personal journey to seek information relating to the people and events that may be hidden within the history of their communities. Living in the past need not be a character flaw; it can be a remarkable and rewarding journey!

Acknowledgements

The author is deeply indebted to the following individuals and organizations for their contributions and support of this project: the Alabama Department of Archives and History (ADAH); the Alabama Power Company Archives (APCA); Glenn Littleton, Thorsby Historical Preservation Museum (THPM); Maplesville Historical Society (MHS); Derric Scott, Chilton County Historical Society (CCHS); Becky Tucker, Chilton County News; Mayor Jeff Mims and the City of Clanton, Alabama; Meghan and Wes Kelly, Clanton First United Methodist Church; and Tim Prince, Brandy Clackley and Joyanna Love of the *Clanton Advertiser* for their support in documenting the history of Chilton County.

The author is especially grateful to Joe Gartrell, acquisitions editor, and Zoe Ames, copy editor, at The History Press, for their guidance, suggestions and many contributions in making this project a reality.

The author gratefully acknowledges the patience, understanding and assistance of the director and staff of the Chilton-Clanton Public Library.

Introduction

In 1998, the Music Corporation of America released the recording *Peaches and Possums: To Clanton, Alabama with Love*, by comedian Jerry Clower. Born in Liberty, Mississippi, the former county agriculture extension agent and fertilizer salesman was known as the Mouth of the South and was a featured performer on the Grand Ole Opry, an American country music concert broadcast weekly from Nashville, Tennessee. Released shortly after his death, *Peaches and Possums: To Clanton, Alabama with Love* was Clower's final recording. Portions of the soundtrack were taped at the Chilton County High School auditorium during one of his last live performances.

Before Jerry Clower brought national notoriety to Chilton County for its principal agricultural export and as the world headquarters of the International Possum Growers and Breeders Association, the county had already attained a diverse and unique historical legacy that began on the western bank of the Coosa River. The Native American village of Pokana Talahassi—or Old Peach Orchard Town, as translated by George Washington Stidham, first chief justice of the Creek Nation—was situated on land that would eventually become Chilton County. This section was part of more than twenty-one million acres of Creek Indian land ceded to the United States government through the Treaty of Fort Jackson in August 1814 following the Battle of Horseshoe Bend, the final engagement of the Creek War.

The opportunities afforded by this newly opened frontier created a migration of settlers who made their way from eastern states by means of wagons loaded only with the supplies necessary to begin their new life. These pioneers secured federal land grants to establish homesteads on fertile farmland located near abundant sources of fresh water. Extensive tracts of timber provided lumber for construction of homes and other buildings. In 1818, one year before Alabama became the twenty-second state admitted to the Union, Autauga and Shelby Counties were established by the territorial legislature within the portion of land acquired through the Treaty of Fort Jackson. These counties would ultimately serve a pivotal role in the creation of Chilton County.

The population of this section would increase dramatically in 1836 following the discovery of gold. In her book *Alabama Gold*, Peggy Walls writes, "The first authenticated discovery of gold in Alabama occurred along Blue Creek and Chestnut Creek in Autauga (now Chilton) County." Even though the search for gold would continue for more than one hundred years, Walls states, "The success of Alabama's gold mining industry depended on the lucky turn of a spade in a sandy creek or the accidental discovery of an unusual rock gleaming from a creek bed." The Alabama gold rush ended in 1849 when prospectors departed the state following the discovery of gold in California.

By 1850, Lower Yellowleaf, an area named for the southern branch of Yellowleaf Creek, a small waterway that meandered aimlessly through the hills and valleys of eastern Autauga County before reaching a confluence with the Coosa River, consisted primarily of yeoman farmers who toiled daily to cultivate small parcels of land.

As a young yeoman farmer in the Lower Yellowleaf section, Alfred Baker worked to develop the land of his new home. Born in March 1828 in the Darlington District of South Carolina, Alfred Baker was a member of one of the pioneer families to settle in the Lower Yellowleaf section. In March 1862, Baker was named justice of the peace of the Chestnut District. Although he opposed the movement that resulted in Alabama becoming one of eleven states to secede from the United States at the beginning of the American Civil War, Baker enlisted as a ninety-day volunteer in the Autauga Rangers Home Guard just three weeks after taking office. After his tour of duty as a second lieutenant, he returned to Autauga County and resumed his position as justice of the peace. In February 1864, mandatory enlistment in the Confederate army was expanded to include all men between seventeen and fifty years of age. As a justice of the peace and possibly because of his Unionist sympathies, Baker requested an exemption from further military service from Governor Thomas H. Watts.

The settlement of Goose Pond consisted primarily of fields, marshes and canebrakes. In May 1871, the Goose Pond post office was renamed the Clanton post office.

The April 1864 letter Alfred Baker sent to Governor Watts requesting the exemption was posted from the small settlement of Ranch, located approximately five miles north of the Chestnut Creek post office. In June 1860, a post office had been established at Ranch with Dr. John Prudence Robinson serving as postmaster. Located on property owned by Joseph Williams of the Mulberry community, the Ranch settlement consisted primarily of fields, marshes and canebrakes, making it an ideal habitat for wild ducks and geese. Located on a section of elevated ground where the

Clanton First Baptist Church would be constructed in 1921, an old log cabin housed the family of William Riley Robinson, the appointed caretaker of the property.

Following the end of the American Civil War, Alfred Baker acquired much of the land that composed the Ranch settlement. Shortly thereafter, the name of the settlement was changed to Goose Pond, a possible reference to the abundance of wild geese that nested among the local ponds and marshes.

In 1868, Alfred Baker was elected to a term of office in the Alabama legislature. According to *The Heritage of Chilton County*, historical records strongly suggest the primary reason Alfred Baker sought a seat in the legislature was to use the political process to create an independent county. Within six months of being elected, Baker was able to achieve his goal. On December 30, 1868, the Alabama legislature adopted an act to create a new county to be called Baker. Created from land acquired from the existing counties of Autauga, Bibb, Perry and Shelby, the new political subdivision was named in honor of its most resolute proponent, becoming the sixty-fifth county to be established in Alabama.

The legislation creating the county of Baker designated five commissioners, all close friends of Alfred Baker or members of the Baker family. The commissioners were tasked to nominate two or more places for a county seat to be selected by a countywide referendum. Affirming their Unionist views, the new county seat selected was named Grantville to honor Ulysses Grant, former commanding general of the U.S. Army and, in November 1868, the president-elect of the United States of America.

In her 1938 *History of Baker County*, Mamie Truett describes Grantville as being located one mile northwest of the Walnut Creek Church in an isolated area with no houses standing within three miles of the courthouse. Builder A.J. Cooper was contracted for the sum of $5,000 to construct a one-room log courthouse, which, according to Truett, appeared more like a kitchen than a courthouse. Presiding judge J.Q. Smith convened court in the single room, which afforded barely enough space to accommodate the parties involved in legal proceedings.

In 1870, two unrelated events would significantly alter the future of Baker County. In November, the final sections of the South and North Alabama Railroad that traversed Baker County were completed. Originally chartered prior to the American Civil War as the Alabama Central Railroad, the rail line was established to connect cotton producers of central Alabama with markets along the Tennessee River. The railroad also serviced the Jefferson County mineral district. The South and North Alabama Railroad entered

Baker County near the community of Mountain Creek and followed a path that connected the towns of Verbena, Barboursville (Coopers), Goose Pond (Clanton), Lomax and Langston Station (Jemison). In May 1871, the South and North Alabama was acquired by the Louisville and Nashville Railroad.

A second event that occurred in 1870 would further impact the future of Baker County: the log courthouse at Grantville was destroyed by a fire of unknown origin. In the months following the destruction of the courthouse, Alfred Baker devoted considerable effort to having the county seat relocated to land he owned in proximity to the railroad. Following an often contentious debate, a referendum was held in April 1871, in which the voters selected the town of Clanton (formerly Goose Pond) as the new center of local government. In 1871, Goose Pond had been renamed for James Holt Clanton (1827–1871) in response to a resolution proposed by the directors of the Louisville and Nashville Railroad and adopted by residents.

Born in Columbia County, Georgia, James Holt Clanton was eight years old when his family moved to Macon County in central Alabama. Clanton would later enroll at the University of Alabama to study law but soon withdrew to serve in the U.S. Army during the Mexican American War (1846–48). Clanton returned to Macon County after the war to complete his study of the law. He attended the Law School of William Parish Chilton, future chief justice of the Alabama Supreme Court. Admitted to the Alabama bar in 1850, Clanton established a law office in the capital city of Montgomery. In 1855, Clanton was elected to represent Montgomery County as a member of the legislature. During the American Civil War, Clanton served as a military officer in the Confederate army until March 1865, when he was seriously wounded and captured at Bluff Springs, Florida. After the war, he returned to his law practice in Montgomery and assumed a leadership position in the Alabama Democratic Party.

Alfred Baker would continue to serve a prominent role during the early history of Chilton County. By December 1874, however, a changing political climate and public accusations of indiscretions committed by Alfred Baker prompted a movement to have his name removed from the county he labored so vigorously to establish. Residents approved a measure to change the name of their county to honor the vaunted and professional statesman William Parish Chilton (1810–1871). A native of Kentucky, Chilton moved to Talladega, Alabama, in 1834 to establish a law practice. He was appointed associate justice of the Alabama Supreme Court in 1848 and, four years later, succeeded Edmund Dargan as chief justice. On January 20, 1871, William Parish Chilton died from injuries sustained from a fall. Although he

Justice of the peace, state legislator and founder of the county that bore his name, Alfred Baker is buried in the Clanton Cemetery.

never resided in Chilton County, his daughter, Jennie (Chilton) Speer, lived in the city of Clanton for many years.

Alfred Baker never regained the prominence he achieved during the early years of his life. Following his death in February 1896, he was buried in the hallowed ground he had graciously donated to the people of Clanton for the establishment of a cemetery. In a sense, it is appropriate that the only memorial chiseled into his marble headstone is the word "Father," for Alfred Baker was a father not only to his family but also to the county that once bore his name.

Since its establishment more than 150 years ago, the growth and development of Chilton County has been significantly influenced by the four pillars of its economy: transportation, hydroelectric power production, timber and agriculture, industries that have provided a livelihood and economic security for generations of residents.

Much of the history of Chilton County is hidden within the stories of these industries, much like the history of a community is hidden within the buildings and monuments that residents often take for granted. These hidden stories represent the mortar that binds together the building blocks of local history, making it stronger and more enduring for future generations.

Hidden History of Chilton County is a collection of those stories, brief glimpses into the histories of individuals, events, buildings and industries that, when woven together, make the overall story of Chilton County stronger and more able to withstand the passage of time. *Hidden History of Chilton County* is the story of the people and events that make the Peach Capital of Alabama a unique and special place, a place that is the heart of Alabama.

Chapter 1

A Celebrated Symbol

Chilton County is known as the Peach Capital of Alabama, and its orchards produce more than two-thirds of the state's leading commercial fruit. The theme of local festivals, parades and pageants, the iconic peach embodies more than an agricultural staple for residents of Chilton County; it is symbolic of a way of life.

A Peach Celebration

During the winter of 1947, community leaders gathered at the Dixie Restaurant on Seventh Street in Clanton for the purpose of forming a committee to organize a celebration to promote the Chilton County peach industry. The *Union Banner* newspaper reported that the meeting was attended by more than forty business owners from Clanton and Thorsby and several bigwigs from Auburn and Birmingham. To lead the effort, J. Archie Ogburn, president of the Bank of Thorsby, was named chairperson of the newly formed committee.

At the time, growers in Chilton County harvested more than five thousand acres of orchards that contained approximately one million peach trees. As the largest producer of the state's leading commercial fruit, Chilton County had earned the distinction of the Peach Capital of Alabama.

Local groups assisting in planning and hosting the festival included the Clanton Kiwanis Club, Clanton Lions Club, Thorsby Civic Club, Thorsby

Businessman's Club and the newly formed Clanton Chamber of Commerce. In planning to make the peach celebration the largest and most colorful event in the history of Chilton County, a steering committee was formed to visit the city of Cullman to gather firsthand information and suggestions relating to organizing a festival. Cullman was selected because of its success in hosting an annual strawberry festival.

In multiple newspaper interviews, festival chairman Ogburn stressed, "The peach festival is not planned as merely a day of festivities. The motives and reasons prompting the occasion add up to one thing and that is to promote and advertise the Chilton County peach industry." With the business interests of Clanton and Thorsby and peach growers throughout the county supporting the festival, Ogburn predicted that the movement would be a walloping success.

To create community spirit and excitement for the upcoming celebration, the festival committee selected "Chilton County Peaches Are Tops!" as a slogan that adorned newspaper advertising, window displays of local merchants and banners throughout Chilton County. In support of the countywide event, all businesses in Clanton, except for drugstores, cafés and filling stations, agreed to close on the day of the festival.

In planning the event, committee members decided that the festival would be held on the grounds of Thorsby Institute. The one-day celebration would include a community picnic and a baseball game between teams from Clanton and Thorsby before concluding with a community dance held at the Thorsby Junior High School. Music for the dance would be provided by the Lewis Simpkins Orchestra. The price of admission was $1.50 for couples and $1.00 for stag attendees. The most highly anticipated activities of the festival included a parade, a peach auction and the crowning of the first queen of the peach festival.

Because the festival committee believed that having a peach queen was as essential as having peaches at a peach festival, chairman Ogburn guaranteed that a peach of a queen would be selected during a banquet and pageant held at Thorsby Institute on the evening preceding the festival. The following day, the queen and her escort would reign over the festivities. To be eligible for the title, contestants were required to be unmarried, between fifteen and twenty-five years of age and

Opposite: An ad for the inaugural Chilton County Peach Festival proclaims, "Chilton County Peaches Are Tops." The one-day festival was held at Thorsby Institute. *THPM.*

Above: A young woman poses near the former railroad depot in Thorsby at the conclusion of the 1947 peach festival parade. *Chilton County Extension Office.*

Essie Lou "Chick" Jones was selected as the 1947 queen of the peach festival during a pageant held at Thorsby Institute. *Chilton County Extension Office.*

the daughter of a Chilton County peach grower. The competition included interviews with pageant judges as well as evening gown and swimsuit competitions. Twelve young women competed for the title.

Judges for the Queen of the Festival competition included L.M. Smith, vice president of the Alabama Power Company; Montgomery city commissioner Tacky Gale; millionaire philanthropist Erskin Ramsey of Birmingham; and Jim Bert, vice president of the First National Bank of Montgomery.

At the conclusion of the competition, fifteen-year-old Essie Lou Jones of the Alpine community was named queen of the Chilton County Peach Festival. A student at the Stanton school, Essie Lou stood five feet, seven inches in height with brown hair and brown eyes. The youngest of eight children, she had been given the nickname "Chick" by her father. To escort the queen, assistant county extension agent Cecil Carlton was selected by acclamation as king of the peach festival. Ironically, Carlton was also known by the nickname "Chick."

During the coronation festivities, homemade tiaras symbolizing royal crowns adorned by a peach were placed on the heads of the queen and king of the festival. The reign of the queen was exceedingly brief, as the title was bestowed for only one day. In a sense, however, the tradition inaugurated by the selection of Essie Lou Jones continues to be reaffirmed after more than seven decades as each successive peach queen is crowned.

On Wednesday, July 16, 1947, numerous out-of-town guests converged on Thorsby for the inaugural peach festival. Representatives of chambers of commerce from Birmingham, Bessemer, Montgomery and Tuscaloosa were present and assisted in organizing activities. State representative C.B. Cox and Senator William A. Gulledge entertained members of the Alabama senate and house of representatives and served as their escorts for the day. Even though these distinguished politicians would be present, event organizers promised speechmaking would be very brief.

The one-day festival began with a parade that originated at the Chilton County High School in Clanton. Led by a military band from Maxwell Field at Montgomery, the parade line included so many vehicles that more than two hours were required to travel the seven-mile route along Highway 31 to Thorsby. Peggy Elders of Gadsden, who had been recently selected as dairy queen of Alabama, led the lengthy line of floats. According to an article in the *Union Banner* newspaper, the parade was "a mile in length and a gorgeous sight to behold." Although intermittent rain showers passed through the area throughout the day, the inclement weather did not dampen the enthusiasm of the participants.

According to newspaper articles describing the event, the first annual Chilton County Peach Festival was an unqualified success. In addition to achieving the goal of creating publicity for the Chilton County peach industry, the festival created a sense of goodwill and community spirit. In a letter to the editor of the *Union Banner*, resident W. Roy Kendrick wrote, "The festival not only showed the peach fruit, but it showed the fruit of good neighborliness and the results of cooperation of several groups of civic-minded people. May this add to the spirit of every civic-minded person in the county, that we may grow closer and be more cooperative in all our undertakings for the betterment of our county."

More than seven decades have passed since a small group of community leaders organized a festival to celebrate the fruit, the growers and the harvests that make Chilton County the Peach Capital of Alabama. From that humble beginning, the Chilton County Peach Festival has grown into a weeklong celebration: a time for the community to come together to remember its past, celebrate the present and preserve a unique way of life for the future. "Chilton County Peaches Are Tops!" is more than a slogan to be proclaimed once each year during the peach festival. It is a statement that defines a county, its people and a way of life.

Peaches for President Truman

With an authoritative voice, auctioneer Tom McCord of the Union Stockyards in Montgomery yelled "Sold!" as he pointed to winning bidder Lee Hornsby during the inaugural peach auction that served as one of the main attractions of the first annual Chilton County Peach Festival. The $250 bid by Hornsby, a state representative from Eclectic, won a bushel of prize-winning Hale Haven peaches produced on the farm of W.H. Lenoir of Maplesville. Earlier in the day, a three-member panel of judges had selected Lenoir's peaches as the best in Chilton County. The blue-ribbon peaches were presented to Hornsby by the queen of the festival, Essie Lou Jones.

The following morning, a committee that included festival queen Essie Lou Jones, king Cecil Carlton, festival chairman Archie Ogburn and county extension agent Red Glasscock loaded the basket of blue-ribbon peaches into an automobile and departed for the Birmingham airport. Upon arrival, the peaches were placed in a reserved seat on an Eastern Airlines flight to Washington. As these were the days before direct, nonstop flights, the Douglas DC-3 aircraft carrying the prize-winning basket of peaches made scheduled stops in Atlanta; Greenville, South Carolina; Winston-Salem and Greensboro, North Carolina; and Richmond, Virginia, before arriving at its destination. During the trip, the special cargo remained under the personal supervision of company president Eddie Rickenbacker, a World War I aviator and recipient of the Medal of Honor.

On Friday July 18, 1947, a delegation including Alabama senators Lister Hill and John Sparkman and Representative Pete Jarman presented the basket containing Chilton County's finest peaches to President Harry Truman during a ceremony at the White House. As a young man, President Truman had worked the family farm in Kansas and for the rest of his life

The prize-winning Hale Haven peaches of the 1947 peach festival were presented to President Harry Truman during a ceremony at the White House. *ADAH.*

maintained an appreciation for agriculture and farming. In a letter to festival chairman Archie Ogburn, President Truman described the peaches as being "as fine as I ever saw." The following morning, the president enjoyed slices of Chilton County peaches on his breakfast cereal.

For the people of Chilton County, the peach represents more than an agricultural and economic staple. In August 1947, the Louisville and Nashville Railroad employee magazine stated, "Peaches represent the very best product of a people not afraid of hard work and planning; a people determined that the whole nation shall someday regard their first festival motto 'Chilton County Peaches Are Tops' as a household phrase."

The Big Peach

The Interstate 65 highway system that traverses Alabama is the most highly traveled thoroughfare in the state. Connecting the Gulf Coast with the Great

Lakes region, the route originates in the port city of Mobile and spans four states before reaching its opposite point of origin in Gary, Indiana. The 366-mile section of Interstate 65 that lies within Alabama connects six of the ten largest cities in the state and is the primary route for vacationers traveling to and from beach resorts along the Gulf Coast.

As travelers pass the northernmost exit ramp leading to downtown Clanton, the county seat of the Peach Capital of Alabama, their attention is immediately drawn to one of the most recognizable landmarks along the 887-mile length of the interstate route: the peach replica water tower known by residents as the Big Peach. Since 1993, this unique structure has captured the attention of visitors and tourists and has provided subliminal encouragement for travelers to exit the interstate to sample the abundant peach-flavored specialty foods and drinks offered by local vendors. One of two such structures in the United States, the second being the Peachoid water tower in Gaffney, South Carolina, the Big Peach was erected as a tribute to Chilton County's most famous product and the growers who produce the state's leading commercial fruit.

The concept of the Big Peach originated in 1992 as the City of Clanton Water and Utility Board identified the need for an additional supply of water to service new homes and businesses, the industrial park at Lomax and the new interstate rest areas under construction nearby. Initially, officials planned only to construct a conventional water storage tower to satisfy the increasing demand. However, the concept of a distinctive design to acknowledge the industry that made Chilton County famous soon became a reality.

A Peach Tower Committee was created to raise the funds necessary to complete the project. Community leaders Lally Bates, Gene Martin, Dan Nolen, Gene Gray, Greg Lollar, Jimmie Harrison and Johnny McKinney agreed to serve as members of the committee. The first obstacle for the newly formed committee to address concerned the design of the new water tower. Because the City of Gaffney held the patent for peachoid-shaped water towers, the group initiated negotiations for approval to utilize the unique design. In subsequent discussions, an agreement was reached to allow the design to be used in Clanton because the term of the patent held by the City of Gaffney was soon scheduled to expire.

In the fall of 1992, the cost of a conventional five-hundred-thousand-gallon water tower was estimated to be $600,000. An additional $500,000 would be required to convert the structure into a peach replica tower. The additional funds required were to be raised through private donations. The State of Alabama initially pledged $85,000 to the project because an eight-inch water line would be routed from the tank to service the nearby interstate rest areas.

In September 1992, the City of Clanton Water and Utility Board and the Clanton City Council voted unanimously to approve construction of the water tower, with the top designed as a golden-yellow peach with a large green leaf. The City of Clanton allocated $600,000 to the project with the balance to be raised by donations from private citizens, corporations, local businesses, civic clubs and other sources. Local media provided periodic updates on fundraising efforts utilizing a simple graphic of a peach-shaped water tower, with the level of water in the tank representing the percentage of funds raised. On November 30, 1992, with sufficient private contributions secured to commence construction, city leaders joined representatives of the Chicago Bridge and Iron Company for a groundbreaking ceremony to initiate construction of Alabama's largest peach.

Founded in 1899, the Chicago Bridge and Iron Company of Norcross, Georgia, was initially involved in the design and construction of wide-span bridges. In the late nineteenth century, the company expanded its services to specialize in the design and construction of elevated water tanks and aboveground storage units for petroleum and refined liquid products. After the corporate headquarters was relocated to Georgia, employees often joked that the Chicago Bridge and Iron Company was no longer a Chicago firm, did not build bridges and no longer used iron, as the name implied.

The company had previously constructed specialty water towers in other localities, including a pineapple-theme tower in Hawaii, baseball and golf ball replica towers at venues across the United States and the Peachoid tower in Gaffney, South Carolina. Construction of the Big Peach in Clanton began in December 1992 as workers started forming the concrete foundation of the tower.

The 120-foot tower is equivalent in height to a twelve-story building. The 500,000-gallon tank has a diameter of sixty feet and weighs approximately 375,000 pounds empty. At full capacity, the weight of the tank increases to more than 4.5 million pounds. The metal leaf that adorns the tower adds approximately 11,000 pounds of weight to the structure. The tower is designed to withstand the force of a one-hundred-mile-an-hour wind.

On a frigid Halloween Day in 1993, peach growers from throughout Chilton County were honored guests for the dedication of the new $1.1 million Peach Tower. The dedication program included a presentation of the tower to the City of Clanton by representatives of the Chicago Bridge

Known by Clanton residents as the Big Peach, the five-hundred-thousand-gallon water storage tank was constructed as a tribute to peach growers in Chilton County.

and Iron Company, remarks by state and local dignitaries and a performance by Southern Pride, a well-known local band.

More than three decades have passed since the idea of a water tower shaped like a peach became a vision and then a reality for the City of Clanton. Today, the Big Peach has remained a constant presence for a new generation of residents who grew into adulthood using water from this most unique and renowned facility. With an average of forty thousand vehicles passing on Interstate 65 each day, the Big Peach is a unique and notable landmark that attracts the attention of travelers from across the United States. For those who live in Clanton, the Big Peach is more than a water tower; it is a symbol of pride and a constant reminder of those who make Chilton County the Peach Capital of Alabama.

Chapter 2

Early Industry

The growth and development of Chilton County has been significantly influenced by the establishment of railroad systems, the agriculture and timber industries and the introduction of hydroelectric power production. Located in the heart of Alabama, Chilton County offers a cordial welcome and wonderful opportunities for industries and agriculture.

A Tale of Two Towns

According to *A History of Chilton County*, produced by the Clanton Study Club in 1927, "Lomax is a little town situated about one mile north of Clanton that was given its historic name in honor of that grand old warrior who so proudly bore it," Colonel Tennant Lomax. Described as a man of towering form and commanding presence, Lomax served in the Third Alabama Regiment during the American Civil War. He lost his life in in 1862 during the first engagement of his military career, the Battle of Seven Pines in Henrico County, Virginia. He died on the day he was to receive a commission as a brigadier general.

Today, motorists traveling along Highway 31 seldom consider that in the late nineteenth century, Lomax rivaled Clanton as the fastest growing and most progressive town in Chilton County. Three years after Baker County, the predecessor to Chilton County, was established, the community of Lomax came within a few votes of becoming the county seat. Following

40 Pages | **CHILTON COUNTY NEWS** | 5 Sections

VOLUME IX   CLANTON, ALABAMA, THURSDAY FEBRUARY 26, 1931   FORTY PAGES   NUMBER 23

CHILTON COUNTY NEWS PRESENTS

CHILTON COUNTY BOOSTER EDITION

PROSPERITY

COMME

TRANSPORTATION

EDUCATION

AGRICULTURE

INDUSTRY

FINANCE

CHILTON COUNTY
In The
Heart of Alabama
Home Of
Hydro-Electric Power
WONDERFUL OPPORTUNITIES
FOR INDUSTRIES
AGRICULTURE AND
DAIRYING
A
CORDIAL WELCOME
AWAITS YOU

CHILTON
COUNTY

Dixie Bee Line Hi-way - 1035 Miles - All Paved

"A Cordial Welcome"

CHICAGO

BIRMINGHAM

CLANTON

CHILTON CO.

MONTGOMERY

MIAMI

The Center of
HYDRO-ELECTRIC PRODUCTION
in
ALABAMA

The February 26, 1931 issue of the *Chilton County News* features the wonderful opportunities for industries and agriculture in the Heart of Alabama. *Chilton County News.*

The Lomax community was named for Colonel Tennant Lomax, who served in the Third Alabama Regiment during the American Civil War. *ADAH.*

a fire that destroyed the first courthouse at Grantville, voters submitted ballots in April 1871 in a referendum to determine the location of the new courthouse. Four communities were included on the ballot: Benson (Isabella), Clanton (formerly known as Goose Pond), Lomax and Verbena. At the completion of two ballots, Clanton was selected by a narrow margin as the new county seat of Baker County.

When rail service was inaugurated through the county by the Louisville and Nashville Railroad, the locomotive engineers complained of the double curve and steep grade near the Clanton depot that made it difficult to start and stop the train. In response, railroad officials began scheduling trains to stop at Lomax, recently modernized with a new rail depot and telegraph station. The Lomax depot soon became the delivery point for passengers and freight bound for Clanton. Transportation by horse-drawn wagon would then be required to transport any passengers or cargo destined for Clanton. For many years, Clanton remained only a flag stop, and mailbags were contemptuously thrown onto the depot platform from the passing trains.

As the community of Lomax continued to grow, a post office was added, and a beautiful hotel was constructed on the hill overlooking the rail station. In 1916, the Vida Lumber Company established a mill in Lomax that produced seventy-five thousand board feet of lumber each day.

In time, however, Clanton grew to such proportions that officials of the Louisville and Nashville Railroad relented and committed the funds necessary to straighten the curves, level the grade and construct sidetracks near the Clanton depot. An agent and a telegraph officer were soon assigned to Clanton, and passengers and freight began arriving on a regular schedule.

The triumph of the town of Clanton over Lomax inspired a poem written by a local resident and published in the December 11, 1910 issue of the *Montgomery Advertiser.*

Clanton capped the climax,
When she grew ahead of Lomax;
The railroad tried to drown us,
But determined folks then found us;
They need not think a hold like that,
Could beat us to the tank;
And Lomax now lies upon the shelf,
And this town is the one to thank.

Today, the city limits of Clanton encompass a part of the former Lomax community. The depot, post office and hotel that made Lomax a thriving community have long ago faded into history. But the area north of Clanton still proclaims the historic name of that grand old warrior who so proudly bore it.

A Magic Carpet Made of Steel

The 1971 ballad "City of New Orleans," by Steve Goodman, is a nostalgic and bittersweet remembrance of the passing of the era of the railroad. The lyrics describe a trip on the Illinois Central Railroad's City of New Orleans, a passenger train consisting of fifteen cars and fifteen restless riders, three conductors and twenty-five sacks of mail rolling along a magic carpet made of steel.

Magic carpets made of steel would have a significant impact on the early development and history of Chilton County. Not unlike present-day interstate highway systems, railroads were the primary means to transport people and products, attracting economic development to communities along their path. The first railroad system to be established in the section that would become Chilton County was the Alabama and Tennessee River Railroad. Incorporated in 1848, the line was created to connect the city of Selma to the Tennessee and Coosa Railroad at a point along the Tennessee River.

The section of rail from Plantersville to Montevallo was routed through the small settlement of Cuba, three miles west of Maplesville. To take advantage of the economic opportunities created by this new transportation system, merchants from Maplesville began relocating to sites convenient to the railroad. In time, the town of Maplesville would be reborn along the railway that traversed the eastern section of Bibb County, land that in 1868 would become Baker and, subsequently, Chilton County.

During the American Civil War, the Alabama and Tennessee River Railroad was utilized to transport iron ore from the mineral belt of central Alabama to the Confederate military arsenal in Selma to produce munitions and weapons. On April 1, 1865, Union troops under the command of General James Wilson made their way south along the Selma Road that followed the path of the Alabama and Tennessee River Railroad. The purpose of their mission was the destruction of the Selma arsenal. After burning the rail depot at Maplesville, Wilson's army engaged the mounted cavalry of General Nathan Bedford Forest near the junction of the Selma and Old Maplesville Roads. According to the book *Wilson's Raid* by Russell Blount Jr., "The ensuing struggle was one of the most vicious hand-to-hand fights between calvary soldiers during the war." Known as the Battle of Ebenezer Church, the engagement was the sole battle to be fought on land that would become Chilton County and represents one of the final skirmishes of the American Civil War.

In 1883, Edward Gregory and Richard Coe of Selma recognized economic opportunity created by the presence of the railroad. The business partners purchased eighty acres of land located on the east side of the rail

The Stanton post office served the residents of the once-thriving community for more than fifty years.

line south of Maplesville and formed the Gregory-Coe Lumber Company. According to *A History of Chilton County*, produced by the Clanton Study Club, Gregory and Coe laid out streets for a village, and quickly, the little town of Stanton came into being.

The village soon became a station on the Selma, Rome and Dalton Railroad, formerly the Alabama and Tennessee River Railroad, and was named for assistant railroad superintendent Myron Stanton, who was fatally injured in a railroad accident. Edward Gregory, founding partner of the Gregory-Coe Lumber Company, would become the first postmaster of Stanton.

Almost two centuries have passed since the first steel rails appeared across the land that would become Chilton County. Like the strands of a spiderweb, these steel rails would spread across the county, becoming a catalyst in the establishment of new towns and communities along their path; serving as a lifeline to remote mill towns that were created, thrived for a time and then vanished without a trace; and surpassing horse-drawn wagons as a primary means of transportation, only to be ultimately replaced by automobiles speeding along four-lane interstate highways. Through it all, the magic carpet made of steel has prevailed as a symbol of strength, stability and continuity in a rapidly changing and often chaotic world.

The Old Reliable

With one long blast of the whistle, the engineer of the No. 2 train signaled its arrival at the Louisville and Nashville (L&N) Railroad depot in Clanton. As the train lurched to a stop, passengers began making their way to the loading platform to embrace relatives, meet business acquaintances or take the first step in making Chilton County their new home. On the freight platform, workers quickly began loading boxcars with peaches, truck crops or cotton for shipment to markets throughout the United States. During the early twentieth century, this scene was not unique to Clanton. It was repeated daily at railroad depots in Verbena, Mountain Creek, Thorsby, Jemison and Maplesville.

In February 1854, the state legislature approved the charter of a new rail system, the Alabama Central Railroad, to operate between the state capital of Montgomery and Decatur in north Alabama. The route was created to connect the cotton producers of central Alabama with markets and textile manufacturers in the Tennessee River region.

The establishment of rail systems in Baker and, subsequently, Chilton County significantly affected the growth and development of communities along their routes. *ADAH.*

The proposed right-of-way traversed the eastern section of Autauga County, an area that would become Baker and subsequently Chilton County. From the outset, financial difficulties created extensive delays in completing the route. In January 1861, the project was halted when the state legislature voted to allow Alabama to secede from the Union of States at the beginning of the American Civil War.

Following the war, the South and North Alabama Railroad was chartered to provide service along the previously proposed route. In 1871, after experiencing financial difficulties, the South and North Alabama was acquired by the L&N Railroad. Known as the Old Reliable, the L&N Railroad would have an immediate effect on the development of towns and communities in Chilton County. Depots, hotels and other businesses were established at Mountain Creek, Verbena, Cooper's Station, Lomax and Jemison to accommodate passengers and freight being transported to and from the county. The railroad also played a significant role in the establishment of the county seat of Clanton. After the county's first courthouse at Grantville was destroyed by fire in 1870, voters in Baker County approved a referendum to move the county seat to Clanton, formerly known as Goose Pond. Convenient access to rail transportation resulted in the town of Clanton becoming a center of business and industry. The new courthouse, a railroad depot, businesses and a hotel were established along Second Avenue North, the main street of Clanton.

The railroad was also an essential element that contributed to the town of Verbena becoming a resort area for affluent families of the Montgomery River region. Rail transportation provided a convenient means of escaping the oppressive summertime heat of the river region to enjoy the fresh air prevalent in the higher elevations of Chilton County. The climate was considered so recuperative that many families traveled by train to Verbena each summer seeking refuge from recurring epidemics of yellow fever. Growth generated by the railroad during this period made Verbena the largest community in Chilton County.

By 1880, lumber companies had become the predominant industry in Chilton County. These operations utilized hundreds of miles of rail lines to transport harvested timber to the mills for processing. Finished products were loaded onto freight cars of the L&N Railroad for distribution to customers throughout the United States. Equally important, transportation of materials and supplies for construction of Lay and Mitchell hydroelectric dams would have not been possible without access to the railroad.

The railroad promoted economic development in other ways. According to Wayne Cline, author of *Alabama Railroads*, the L&N Railroad invested large sums of money to attract settlers to remote areas along its route through Alabama. In 1895, Theodore Thorson traveled to Alabama in search of a region having a mild climate and land suitable for the cultivation of vegetables, fruits and vineyards.

Arriving in Chilton County, Thorsen inspected parcels of land located near the railroad depot at Strasburgh, a settlement located approximately three miles north of the Lomax community. After evaluating the climate, length of the growing season and availability of land, Thorsen decided the region was ideal for realizing his dream of creating a community of craftsmen, merchants and farmers. The new community became Thorsby.

Thorson marketed five- and ten-acre lots to families of Scandinavian and Norwegian heritage. A modern hotel was constructed to provide temporary lodging for new arrivals. Families could rent a boxcar from the railroad for thirty dollars to ship household furnishings to their new home.

Construction of U.S. Highway 31 marked the beginning of the decline of rail travel in Chilton County. Trains with exotic names like the Hummingbird and Pan American no longer stopped at depots painted in the distinctive green of the L&N line. Over time, most of the depot buildings were boarded

The former Louisville and Nashville Railroad depot in Clanton is a reminder of the bygone days of rail travel.

up and eventually torn down, replaced by bus and automobile service stations established along the new highway.

A long blast of the whistle no longer announces the arrival of the Louisville and Nashville No. 2 train at the Clanton depot. Yet the old depot building still stands as a testament to the passage of time and the role served by the Old Reliable during the 150-year history of Chilton County.

The Depot

In the predawn stillness of January 27, 1911, a sharp blast from the whistle of a southbound Southern Railway freight train alerted residents of Maplesville that a fire was consuming the building of local merchant R.H. Martin. Awakened by the alarm, members of the community valiantly attempted to extinguish the flames, but the fire spread quickly and engulfed the wood-frame structures nearby.

Ironically, the Southern Railway depot was one of the buildings consumed by the fire. Rebuilt the following year, the depot building has become an

Constructed in 1912, the Southern Railway depot in Maplesville has served the community for more than one hundred years. *MHS.*

iconic structure that represents the history of Maplesville and its relationship with the railroad.

According to *Maplesville: The Town and The People*, the first railroad depot to serve the community that would become Maplesville was constructed about 1853 in conjunction with the establishment of the Alabama and Tennessee River Railroad. The original town of Maplesville was situated three miles to the east of new rail line. As merchants and residents began relocating to sites near the railroad, the old Maplesville community faded away, and the town was reborn in proximity to the depot.

The original depot was destroyed when soldiers of the Union army burned the building during their advance on the Confederate arsenal and foundry at Selma. Rebuilt after the war, the depot served not only as a center of business and commerce but also as a place for families to spend a leisurely Sunday afternoon watching the trains pass.

Beginning in the late nineteenth century, the town of Maplesville became the crossing point of two rail systems, the Gulf, Mobile and Ohio and the Southern Railway. The relationship between the people of Maplesville and the railroad companies would span more than seventy-five years. This relationship was beneficial for the railroad and residents of the town.

Whenever a special group of passengers traveling on the Gulf, Mobile and Ohio passed through Maplesville, the local station agent would contact Gladys Nix of the Green Roof Café. Known for having the best home-cooked meals along the route, Nix would prepare as many as forty hot lunches for the passengers.

When the train arrived, Nix would deliver the lunches to the depot. For the price of forty cents, each meal included a cup of fruit juice. In an era before the use of paper products became common, lunch would be served on dishes, with silverware provided. The conductor would return the dishes to Nix on the return trip the next day.

Before the Maplesville High School was accredited, students who lived along the Southern Railway could ride the train to attend classes at Dallas County High School in Plantersville. The No. 19 train southbound from Maplesville arrived each morning at 9:00 a.m. In the afternoon, students would return home on the northbound service. For the sum of $4.89, students could purchase a ticket book valid for thirty days of travel between the towns. To accommodate the students who traveled by train, the school

An iconic landmark, the former Southern Railway depot in Maplesville is currently utilized as a recreation center for senior citizens.

scheduled a study hall for local students as the first class of the morning. Academic classes began after the train from Maplesville arrived. Should a student miss the train home, an overnight stay with relatives or families of friends would be arranged.

Today, the only remnant of the Gulf, Mobile and Ohio Railroad is an abandoned rail bed, while the once proud black-and-white styling of the Southern Railway has been lost in a series of mergers and consolidations. The former Southern Railway depot has been reborn as a senior citizen's center in the town it has served for more than one hundred years. For visitors to the senior center, the sharp blast of the horn of an approaching freight train often revives memories of bygone days when trains of the Southern Railway signaled their arrival at the station.

The Vida Lumber Company

In November 1916, an article in the *Union Banner* newspaper informed readers that the Vida Lumber Company, one of the largest manufacturers of yellow pine lumber in Alabama, had purchased a large tract of timber located along the hills of east Chilton County near the Coosa River. The article also indicated that the company was seeking a new site for their big mill plant.

According to Thomas Lawson, author of *Logging Railroads of Alabama*, the Vida Lumber Company was organized in 1910 when investors purchased the assets of the Cruise-Splawn Lumber Company, located near the community of Vida in Autauga County. By late 1916, the company had cut out their supply of timber in Autauga County and wanted to relocate their logging operations to the abundant pine forests of Chilton County.

Editorials in the *Union Banner* newspaper promoted the recruitment of the Vida Lumber Company as an enterprise that Clanton could not afford to lose. The newspaper implored those citizens who could offer inducements for the location of the mill there to get busy performing their part in bringing this good enterprise to Clanton.

In January 1917, representatives of the Vida Lumber Company announced plans to construct the new mill on a site located north of Clanton at Lomax. After relocating equipment previously used at the mill site at Vida, the company invested an additional $75,000, equivalent to $1.5 million in 2022, to build the mill. Six massive coal-fired boilers were erected to produce steam power to operate the large saws and other equipment. More than 150 houses were constructed to accommodate workers and their families. Food and other necessities could be purchased at the mill commissary by exchanging scrip that was used to pay workers instead of government-issued currency.

In July 1917, the mill at Lomax began processing harvested timber with a daily capacity of seventy-five thousand board feet. For the next seven years, the Vida Lumber Company remained one of the most successful industries in Chilton County.

In addition to the sawmill, a narrow-gauge railroad, known as a tram or dinky line, was constructed to transport harvested timber from logging operations along the Coosa River to the mill site. The raw timber was transported to the mill by four steam-powered locomotives and approximately thirty railcars operating along twenty-five miles of track. Originating from a spur that connected to the main line of the Louisville and Nashville Railroad at Lomax, the tram line proceeded east to a point near the old turpentine still near the mouth of Walnut Creek on the Coosa River. The tram line included two rail spurs; the Margaret Jones Spur, which passed over the mountain to the north, and a southern line that crossed Refuge Road near the Baptist church and ended at Persimmon Thicket Branch.

Raw timber was unloaded into the large millpond for storage before being moved to the sawmill for processing. The yellow pine lumber, produced in various lengths, was then placed in one of four large Moore moist-air type kilns, measuring 20 feet in width by 104 feet in length, for drying.

In March 1918, an article in the *Union Banner* reported, "Improvements being done by the Vida Lumber Company and the development of the turpentine industry are making Lomax assume the outward appearance of a city." The old post office at Lomax was again put into operation after a lapse of several years because the influx of people the big mill brought to the little town. To accommodate the increasing number of visitors, the company announced that a large hotel would be constructed that would be a model of its kind.

The hotel was constructed on top of a hill overlooking the mill and was composed of sixteen guest rooms located on two levels. The second floor was accessed by a central staircase with four rooms located on each side of the upstairs landing. Each guest room was identified by a decorative brass number affixed to the door.

Employment at the mill often proved to be hazardous. Articles in the *Union Banner* reported that local doctors were often called to the mill to treat workers injured by saws and other machinery. Often, these injuries were so severe that victims had to be transported to a Montgomery hospital for amputation of an arm or leg. Accidents were not limited to the mill site. In September 1921, a fire of unknown origin destroyed the school building in the Pinedale Community. Residents speculated that since the tram line of the Vida Lumber Company ran within sixty feet of the building, the fire was started by a spark from the smokestack of a passing log train.

At noon on Saturdays, the shrill blast of the mill's steam whistle signaled the end of the long work week. During the summer months, workers and their families would often spend the afternoon cheering for the company baseball team. In one contest against Thorsby Institute, the lumbermen of Vida were routed by a score of 25–12 in seven innings. Reporting on the game, a writer for the *Union Banner* described the Vida team as really being able to get around the field—but seldom to where the ball was hit.

The economic prosperity created by the Vida Lumber Company at Lomax would last only as long as the abundant supply of yellow pine timber obtained from large tracts of land along the Coosa River. By the spring of 1923, that supply and the economic prosperity it created came to an end.

In July 1923, the *Union Banner* published a series of advertisements offering for sale various assets of the Vida Lumber Company. One advertisement read, "On account of moving the mill, we have about 150 houses for sale cheap. Anyone wanting a bargain should call to see us at once." A second ad offered "six head of fine oxen at a very reasonable figure." An article included on the front page of the same edition offered a brief explanation of the sale of the assets: "The big mill of Vida Lumber Company, which has been running at Lomax for the past seven years, is closed. Arrangements are being made to move the mill to a site west of Maplesville along the Mobile and Ohio Railroad. The mill closed because tracts of timber along the Coosa River had been cut out, the supply of Yellow Pine exhausted." Most of the men employed at the mill had been transferred to Leeds, Alabama, where the company had recently purchased one of the most fully equipped lumber mills in the state.

Closure of the mill had an immediate and adverse effect on the Lomax community. The post office and the Vida Hotel soon closed, while the locomotives and cars used on the logging railroad sat idle along the abandoned rail spur. Although the Vida Lumber Company was no longer part of the Lomax community, some of the buildings and structures of the former mill remained intact.

As a child, Thomas Davis moved with his family to live in the former Vida Hotel. His father, a one-mule farmer, rented land across the railroad tracks to raise cotton. Living in the old hotel was an adventure for the young Thomas. He fondly recalls the large front porch, where his mother would cut the children's hair on Saturday mornings using manual clippers.

On the upper level, a large veranda with an ornate banister could be accessed from the top of the wide staircase. Thomas and his younger brother discovered that during the fall, when the trees were bare of leaves, they could watch movies being projected on the screen of the Clanton Drive-In Theatre using a single lens spyglass. With no audible sound, the plots of the movies were subject to interpretation and left much to the imagination.

Although the old hotel had running cold water, morning coffee and winter baths required water heated on a wood stove. Because Thomas's father also operated a small sawmill, known as a peckerwood mill, slabs were used as fuel for the stove. The old hotel did not have the luxury of indoor toilets.

The old mill site was always a wonderful place for fun and adventure. Thomas and his friends would often walk the rail lines looking for detonators, commonly known as torpedoes. These devices were developed as a warning signal for railroad engineers. Secured to the top of the rail by lead straps, the torpedoes were designed to explode, emitting a loud noise, as the weight of the train compressed them.

This concrete foundation is one of the last remnants of the Vida Lumber Company at Lomax.

Thomas and his friends would commandeer the torpedoes and take them to the old mill site. They would place a torpedo at the bottom of one of the large concrete foundations that once supported the massive steam engines that powered the mill. A designated member of the group would climb to the top of the eight-foot foundation and drop bricks on the torpedo to produce a loud bang. After the excitement of exploding rail torpedoes abated, the group would invent other games to be played along the levee and abutments surrounding the log pond.

Today, with the exception of an occasional rusted rail spike found buried along the old rail line and the man-made levee that once formed a section of the log pond, little remains of the mill that was once the largest industry in Chilton County. The high-pitched sound of large saws transforming yellow pine timber into lumber have been silent for almost a century, carried away by the passage of time and transformed into the history of our past.

Life in a Sawmill Town

Each weekday morning at four o'clock, four long blasts from the steam whistle of the E.E. Jackson Lumber Company would echo across the small mill town of Riderville. Affectionately known as Old Betsy, the whistle served as a wake-up call to summon workers for another day harvesting and processing timber from abundant tracts of longleaf pine trees in southwest Chilton County.

Located two miles north of Plantersville, the mill town of Riderville was named for its first postmaster, Noah H. Rider, who also served as one of the founders of the E.E. Jackson Lumber Company. Incorporated in Alabama in 1896, the company was named for lumberman and former governor of Maryland E.E. Jackson.

Like other mill towns in the county, Riderville was a self-contained community that included a church, commissary, physician's office and school. The Riderville Hotel, constructed for the convenience of visitors arriving on the company's two-coach passenger and mail train, was conveniently located near the main line of the Southern Railway.

The E.E. Jackson Lumber Company utilized a short line railroad system to transport harvested timber to the mill site for processing. These logging railroads extended for miles into areas described as vast oceans of trees stretching without a break in every direction as far as the eye could see. A

The Gregory-Coe Lumber Company of Stanton was incorporated in August 1883 and utilized a logging railroad to transport raw materials to the mill. *MHS.*

section of timber, extending one mile to either side of the rail line, would be harvested by workers using axes and handsaws. The timber would then be dragged from the work site to the railcars by a team of oxen or mules.

The loaded railcars would be pulled to the mill site by a Lima Locomotive Works Shay engine. After processing, the finished lumber products were loaded onto another railcar and transferred to the main line of the Southern Railway to be transported to distant markets. The E.E. Jackson rail system was part of the Riderville, Centerville and Blocton Railroad. This short line rail system consisted of eight locomotives and approximately one hundred railcars operating on thirty-five miles of track. From 1880 until 1920, fifteen lumber companies within Chilton County utilized short line rail systems for logging operations.

Employees of the E.E. Jackson Lumber Company were paid in scrip. The scrip was a substitute for government-issued currency and was used to purchase food, dry goods and other items from the mill commissary. Community activities such as picnics and holiday celebrations were eagerly anticipated events. Often, gondola railcars normally utilized to transport coal for the mill's steam boiler would be pulled by a company locomotive to transport workers, their families and friends to a scenic spot along the rail line for a day of recreation. The selected spot would typically be near a pond or creek to provide relief from the summertime heat.

By 1916, the supply of timber in the southern section of Chilton County had been exhausted. The mill at Riderville was disassembled and moved to the new settlement of Riderwood in Choctaw County. Before the integration of forestry management practices, the Twin Tree Lumber Company at Maplesville, Gregory-Coe at Stanton, the Clear Creek Lumber Company at Ocampo and other large sawmill companies would operate only as long as they had access to abundant supplies of timber. Once that commodity was exhausted, the companies would be relocated or fade into history.

Today, there are no highway signs pointing the way to Riderville. The predawn blasts of Old Betsy have been silent for more than a century. Even though the concept of the mill town would briefly reappear before vanishing forever in Chilton County, the bygone era of the sawmill town represents a remarkable chapter in the history of our county and its people.

The Log Train

During the late nineteenth century, the sound of steam-powered locomotives laboring under heavy loads echoed through the vast pine forests of Chilton County. Clouds of smoke billowed from the massive engines as they struggled to pull railcars heavily loaded with timber through rugged hills and river bottoms along a vast complex of steel rail lines that traversed the county.

The establishment of rail systems to transport timber from logging camps to the sawmills was the result of a rapid expansion of the lumber industry following the end of the American Civil War. Large lumber companies operating in Chilton County depended on an uninterrupted supply of timber to meet the needs of customers throughout the southeast. As tracts of timber near the sawmills were depleted, or cut out, new timber had to be transported over greater distances. Prior to the development of roadways and trucks capable of transporting massive quantities of freight, railroads provided the most dependable and efficient means of transporting timber.

The log trains would make multiple trips to the logging camps each day to retrieve loads of timber for the sawmill. In the camps, two-man teams used crosscut saws or axes to harvest trees. The cut timber would be dragged by oxen or mule to the spur that connected to the main rail line leading to the sawmill. At the railhead, logs would be loaded onto the train car by a steam loader or manual labor.

The E.E. Jackson Lumber Company was one of fifteen timber companies in Chilton County that utilized rail systems to transport harvested timber. *ADAH.*

The normal workday in the logging camps began at dawn and ended at sunset. Workers lived in large wooden camp cars mounted on railroad wheels that could be transported from site to site as logging operations progressed. Because logging camps were in remote and isolated areas, log trains were often the only connection workers had with the outside world. On Saturdays, the sight of an old boxcar connected to the end of the train was cause for celebration, as it signaled the arrival of supplies and the payroll. The boxcar also provided a ride back to town for workers to rejoin their families or to spend a luxurious night in a hotel in Jemison, Clanton or Verbena.

Lumber companies often created separate names for their railroad operations. Incorporated in 1884, L. J. Hand and Company of Jemison operated the Piney Woods Central. The Baldwin and Shay engines that pulled massive carloads of timber were also personalized with the names of notable individuals, like the Charles A. Sands, operated by the Twin Tree Lumber Company at Maplesville.

According to *Logging Railroads of Alabama* by Thomas Lawson Jr., overloaded trains, temporary track, collapsed trestles, derailments and boiler explosions created an extremely dangerous work environment along the rail lines. As the railroads operated in heavily forested areas, wildlife also posed a threat to the log trains and crews. A collision with a stray cow, deer or wild hog could easily derail the train.

Although operators of logging railroads prohibited alcohol consumption on the job, many train crews kept a jug of strong moonshine on hand to treat rattlesnake bites and other injuries. Snakes also had a nasty habit of dropping onto the trains from overhanging limbs, creating a mass evacuation of those workers riding on top of the log cars.

Logging railroads began to disappear during the early years of the twentieth century as sawmills cut out leased timberland or went bankrupt due to declining lumber markets. After sitting idle for many years, the once proud engines that pulled the log trains were cut up and scrapped for metal needed during the Second World War.

Although the tracks have been gone for almost one hundred years, strolling through the woods of Chilton County, it is not uncommon to find a rail spike that seems out of place or an overgrown track bed leading deep into the forest, reminders of a time when a billowing cloud of smoke announced the approach of a log train bound for the sawmill.

Turpentine, the Magic Elixir

During a visit to central Alabama in 1828, British naval officer Basil Hall described the region as a vast ocean of trees, stretching without a break in every direction, as far as the eye could see. The vast ocean of trees that so impressed Hall were longleaf pines, a natural resource that has been a vital component of the local economy since the formative years of Chilton County.

Lumber from these longleaf pine trees was used by early settlers to construct houses, churches, barns and other structures. In January 1880, the Pratt Sawmill Company of Verbena, the first such enterprise to be incorporated in Alabama, became the first sawmill in Chilton County to process longleaf pine into lumber for shipment to markets outside of the state.

In December 1916, the longleaf pine forests of Chilton County became a valuable economic resource for another reason. A front-page article in the *Union Banner* informed readers, "The Oden-Elliott Lumber Company has transferred more than 11,000 acres of timberland in Chilton County to the new Alabama Turpentine Company."

Turpentine is an oil created by the distillation of tree resin. Early settlers considered turpentine an elixir for a variety of ailments, an antiseptic used

Diagonal cuts were made in the trunks of longleaf pine trees to allow resin to drain into the collection box to produce turpentine oil.

to heal wounds, a treatment for lice and a means to kill intestinal parasites and to soothe nasal conditions and sore throats. In the home, this magic elixir was also used as a solvent and as an inexpensive alternative fuel for oil-burning lamps.

To obtain this valuable oil, workers cut a box into the base of a pine tree to trap the resin. Diagonal cuts were then made in the trunk of the tree above the box. This allowed the resin to drain into a container placed in the box. After the box and cuts were completed, the exposed wood of the tree was thought to resemble the facial features of a cat; the effect was known as a cat-face cut.

During the distillation process, workers used a large vat over an open fire to heat the resin to boiling temperature. The vapor created flowed through a tube at the top of the vat, where it condensed and dripped into a collection barrel. After the turpentine and water separated, workers skimmed the turpentine from the surface of the mixture.

Operating from a plant located ten miles east of Clanton on the Coosa River, the Alabama Turpentine Company utilized convict labor, leased from Alabama prisons, to collect and process the turpentine. A reporter for the *Union Banner* observed that "more than one-hundred convicts have been working at the plant for several weeks. A huge stockade has been erected for their retention and a pack of bloodhounds is kept for the recovery of any convict who might take a voluntary leave of absence."

The turpentine was transported from the plant by large trucks having a capacity of approximately fifteen barrels. In Clanton, the turpentine was loaded into boxcars of the Louisville and Nashville Railroad for delivery to customers along the Eastern Seaboard.

The history of the turpentine industry in Chilton County was relatively brief, lasting only as long as the extensive tracts of longleaf pines. After cutting out large tracts of timber, lumber companies would relocate their operations to virgin forests that provided new supplies of raw material, leaving only the memory and aroma of freshly cut longleaf pine trees and the magic elixir they provided.

The Dam at Lock 12

On a Saturday afternoon in November 1929, more than two thousand people braved frigid temperatures and dreary skies to travel to a point along the Coosa River to attend the dedication ceremony of the first hydroelectric dam to be constructed in Alabama. The festivities included a barbecue lunch and speeches by politicians and civic leaders. The Goodyear blimp *Vigilant* floated lazily overhead throughout the afternoon.

Originally known as the Dam at Lock 12, the structure was dedicated in honor of William Patrick Lay, founder and first president of the Alabama Power Company. In the book *Putting Loafing Streams to Work*, author Harvey Jackson III describes Lay as a third-generation river man and pioneer in electrical power production in Alabama. In 1906, Lay founded the Alabama Power Company to pursue his dream of harnessing the power of the river to produce electricity on a scale greater than residents of Alabama had ever known.

The site selected by William Lay for the first hydroelectric dam in Alabama was a remote spot on the Coosa River located eleven miles east of Clanton. It was described as a rapids-infested site between high bluffs surrounded by forests. The Army Corps of Engineers originally proposed construction of a lock at the site as part of a project to open the river to navigation. However, the cost of making the river navigable was determined to be excessive, and the plan was abandoned.

In March 1907, President Theodore Roosevelt signed legislation approving construction of the dam proposed by William Lay. The approval included a March 1914 deadline for completion of the project. Construction began in 1912 following a change in company management in which William Patrick Lay placed the good name and destiny of the Alabama Power Company into the capable hands of James Mitchell and Montgomery attorney Thomas W. Martin. Surveys indicated that the reservoir created by the dam would cover 4,700 acres of land consisting of forests, creek-bottom farms and areas previously cleared of trees by timber companies.

By 1913, construction of the all-concrete dam employed more than 1,500 workers, who were housed in a village located near the construction site. In addition to housing, the village included medical, recreational and religious facilities. During the peak of construction, the village became the largest population center between Montgomery and Birmingham.

Construction materials were transported to the site along a rail spur originally constructed by the Clear Creek Lumber Company. The spur, twenty-two miles in length, originated at the main Louisville and Nashville rail line at Ocampo and crossed forty-five trestles as it traversed the hilly terrain to the construction site. The project contractor, the MacArthur Brothers Company of New York, established two quarries near the project site to supply material for the 343,985 cubic yards of concrete required

More than 1,500 workers were employed during construction of the hydroelectric dam at Lock 12. *APCA.*

Completed in December 1913, the hydroelectric dam at Lock 12 was named in honor of William Patrick Lay, founder of the Alabama Power Company.

to build the dam. At the time, the Dam at Lock 12 was the largest, most complex and most expensive construction project in the state of Alabama.

In 1923, the Alabama Power Company completed a second hydroelectric dam project in Chilton County. Located twelve miles downstream in an area known as Duncan's Riffle, Mitchell Dam was dedicated in honor of James Mitchell, who succeeded William Patrick Lay as president of the Alabama Power Company.

Harvey Jackson III suggests that construction of the hydroelectric dams on the Coosa River was a turning point, not only for Chilton County but also for the state of Alabama. "When their turbines began spinning and electricity began to flow to farms, towns and cities, Alabama moved from the nineteenth into the twentieth century. The state and its people would never be the same."

THE VILLAGE AT DUNCAN'S RIFFLE

Situated between the Narrows and Hell's Gap, Duncan's Riffle was considered one of the most isolated and least accessible sections along the Coosa River. Entering Chilton County, the river crossed a ragged, irregular fall line that included reefs, shoals and rapids. In *Rivers of History*, author Harvey Jackson III writes, "Through this section, the river raised a protesting roar that could be heard from miles away." Surprisingly, the isolated wilderness of Duncan's Riffle would, for a brief period, become one of the largest and most cosmopolitan communities located between Birmingham and Montgomery.

In July 1921, workers of the Dixie Construction Company, a subsidiary of the Alabama Power Company, began construction of a second hydroelectric dam on the Coosa River in Chilton County. The first dam, completed in 1914, was located fourteen miles upstream of Duncan's Riffle. Originally known as the Dam at Lock 12, the structure was renamed in November 1929 for William Patrick Lay, the first president of the Alabama Power Company.

Company surveyors and engineers were the first to arrive at the Duncan's Riffle site. These workers initially obtained lodging at the Porter House Hotel in Verbena. Because the Duncan's Riffle site was so isolated, the Alabama Power Company erected a construction camp to provide accommodations for more than two thousand workers and their families. In *Putting Loafing Streams to Work*, Harvey Jackson III describes

The construction village at Duncan's Riffle provided on-site living quarters and a dining hall, infirmary, commissary, school and church for workers and their families. *APCA.*

the living quarters as being designed to harmonize with and enhance the natural scenic beauty of the area, making the workers' village one of the showplaces of the South.

An independent community in every regard, the village included a large commissary that carried an extensive assortment of goods one would expect to find in the better establishments of Clanton and Verbena. Free health care was provided for workers and their families at the modern fifteen-bed infirmary. A school constructed in the village offered courses of instruction identical to those provided to students in nearby community schools.

Transmission lines from the hydroelectric plant at Lock 12 furnished power for lights and appliances in the homes, bunkhouses and offices of the village at Duncan's Riffle during a time electricity was not readily available to most residents of Chilton County. In October 1921, the company newsletter *Powergrams* reported that the village provided most of the conveniences of the city, with none of the congestion.

Recreation was an important aspect of life at Duncan's Riffle. Indoor basketball games and boxing matches were held in the new gymnasium. A baseball team was organized to compete against teams from other communities. During baseball season, it was not unusual for a worker to be hired more for his ability to throw a fastball than his skill as a carpenter.

Mitchell Dam at Duncan's Riffle on the Coosa River was completed in 1923 and was the second hydroelectric project in Chilton County. *APCA.*

This decorative fixture is one of the remnants of the former construction village located at Duncan's Riffle.

This staircase constructed of stones once led to the recreation area of the construction village at Duncan's Riffle.

Dances and other social events were frequently held at the Masonic Hall and were attended by guests from Verbena, Clanton, Birmingham and Montgomery. The Masonic Hall also served as a theater, showing recently released movies three nights each week. On weekends, workers and their families enjoyed picnics, fishing and other outdoor activities in the scenic surroundings along the river. For some, a joyride in one of the construction buckets suspended from cables high above the river was a perfect way to spend a Sunday afternoon.

Completed in August 1923, the new hydroelectric dam was named for James Mitchell, former president of the Alabama Power Company. The construction camp was abandoned, and workers of the Dixie Construction Company were relocated to their next project at Cherokee Bluffs in Tallapoosa County.

Almost a century has passed since the rapids of Duncan's Riffle were tamed, transformed into a massive reservoir containing fifty-six billion gallons of water at full pool. Today, little remains of the village that was once the largest and most cosmopolitan community between Birmingham and Montgomery. Yet the view from the observation platform that overlooks the dam and reservoir is a vivid reminder that Lake Mitchell and its surroundings remain one of the showplaces of the South.

The Bee Line Highway

In June 1914, more than five thousand people gathered in a grove near the Masonic Hall in Clanton to attend an Alabama Good Roads Rally, organized to promote development of a new automobile route between Birmingham and Montgomery. An article in the *Union Banner* described Clanton as being in gala attire, with the entire population on hand to welcome out-of-town visitors arriving by automobile, the railroad and horse-drawn wagons.

The rally was sponsored by the Birmingham to Montgomery Highway Association, an organization led by a six-member committee consisting of representatives from Jefferson, Shelby, Chilton, Elmore, Autauga and Montgomery Counties. Chilton County civic leader Lewis Henry Reynolds served as chairman of the association. Following a barbecue lunch, Governor Emmet O'Neal encouraged the assembled crowd to support development of the great automobile speedway between Birmingham and Montgomery.

Prior to the introduction of the automobile, travel from Birmingham to Montgomery by horse-drawn carriage required a minimum of three days under the most favorable conditions. The first scout trip by automobile in 1909 required more than twenty-four hours to complete. Adverse road conditions often made the route impassible or resulted in lengthy delays.

The effort to construct the new highway was part of the proposed Great Lakes to the Gulf Highway that would connect the city of Chicago with the Gulf Coast. The highway would become one of the earliest roads in

Alabama to be established along the most direct route between major cities and to be designed and constructed in compliance with new safety standards that included a roadbed of consistent width and grade.

Completed in 1915, the single-lane gravel road traversed Chilton County along a route parallel to the Louisville and Nashville Railroad. In 1921, the route was designated a "Bee Line Highway," a reference to its straight path between cities. In January 1923, contracts were approved for reconstructing the highway with concrete. The route was straightened, reducing the length of the highway by more than five miles and decreasing the travel time between Birmingham and Montgomery to less than six hours. In May 1928, the last section of concrete was poured at a point near Mountain Creek.

The potential economic benefits of being located on the improved highway caused some lively debates among business proprietors in Clanton, who waged vigorous contests over the most favorable route through the city. The issue was settled in March 1925 when the Clanton City Council granted permission to the Alabama Highway Commission to use Seventh Street as the route of the first federal highway to be established through Clanton and Chilton County.

Construction of the Birmingham to Montgomery Highway commenced in 1914 along a route that paralleled the Louisville and Nashville rail line. *ADAH.*

The Birmingham to Montgomery Highway eventually became Highway 31. Subsequent straightening of the highway eliminated multiple sections of road, making this a bridge to nowhere.

During the same period, the Joint Board on Interstate Highways finalized development of the modern highway numbering system. Routes running north to south were assigned odd numbers, while those running east to west were designated by even numbers. The number 1 or 5 was added to identify main routes. Consequently, the Birmingham to Montgomery Highway became known as Highway 31 on newly introduced road maps.

The economic impact of Highway 31 in Chilton County was equally significant to the establishment of the railroad more than fifty years earlier. Modern motor courts, automobile service stations, restaurants and hotels soon appeared along the route, creating economic growth in the towns of Verbena, Clanton, Thorsby and Jemison. The highway would continue to serve as a major contributor to the local economy for more than thirty years, until the establishment of the Eisenhower Interstate System ushered in the next major shift in the economic and community development of Chilton County.

The Cotton Mill

During the early years of the textile industry, manufacturers of cotton products were primarily located in states throughout New England. By the early twentieth century, however, textile manufacturers recognized that production costs could be significantly reduced by locating mills in the Southeast, where much of the supply of cotton was produced.

In December 1927, a representative of the Alabama Power Company Industrial Department arrived in Clanton with a proposal for community leaders. The Alabama Mills Company, operator of nine cotton mills in the state, was seeking a location for an expansion of its business.

According to the Alabama Power Company representative, the town of Clanton was being considered because of the high character and civic spirit of its citizens, its healthful and equitable climate, splendid labor force and many other natural advantages.

Local financial support was an important aspect of the proposed venture. Probate judge L.H. Reynolds quickly formed a Cotton Mill Committee to review the proposal. Within two weeks, residents purchased more than three hundred subscriptions to raise the $150,000 required to finalize the deal.

The site selected for construction of the new mill was a parcel of land known as the Morgan property. Located one mile northwest of the courthouse, the twenty-six-acre site was situated between the Birmingham to Montgomery Highway and the Louisville and Nashville Railroad near the Willis Tourist Camp.

To accommodate approximately three hundred workers, a mill village consisting of forty-one apartment houses was constructed on the site. In a 1929 *Union Banner* article, the village was described as a modern little city with all conveniences. "The village houses have plenty of bedrooms, a kitchen and running water. They are arranged along newly graded streets and have a comfortable and homey appearance." Because the company agreed to encourage employees to shop in Clanton, the village did not include a commissary.

On December 21, 1929, the Clanton mill turned the first bale of cotton into finished yarn. During the first ten years of operation, more than thirty thousand bales of cotton were processed at the mill. The cotton mill operated on a twenty-four-hour basis, five days each week. During the Second World War, employees of the mill further increased production to meet the demands of the war effort. Mill workers also participated in blood drives, war bond rallies and other patriotic efforts.

Above: This aerial view of the Alabama Mills Clanton division facility shows the mill village, which consisted of forty-one apartment houses constructed for employees.

Left: A memorial erected by the Alabama Mills Clanton division to honor employee Reuben Mims and others who served during the Second World War.

The Alabama Mills Clanton division began operation in December 1929 and operated continuously for more than forty years.

In the book *The Great Eight: The 1975 Cincinnati Reds*, Clanton native and Major League Baseball star Clay Carroll reminisced, "When I was a kid, most of the people in town worked in the cotton mill." He recalled that his father, a mill worker for forty years, put aside enough money from his weekly pay to allow the nine Carroll children to have a Popsicle every Saturday.

In May 1956, the production facilities of the Alabama Mills Company were acquired by Dan River Mills of Danville, Virginia. In August 1977, five decades after the mill was first proposed to community leaders, the management of Dan River Mills announced that it would permanently close the Clanton manufacturing facility because of continuing unprofitable operations. The mill became a victim of textile manufacturers transferring operations to locations outside of the United States to achieve lower production costs.

Today, the former site of the Alabama Mills Company, once Clanton's largest employer, stands as a testament to a time when families left the cotton field to work in the cotton mill as they struggled to survive the dark days of the economic depression.

Chapter 3

Places Remembered

Communities are often defined by the buildings and structures located within their boundaries. With the passing of generations, these local landmarks often change in appearance and identity before ultimately being removed to make space for a new generation. Not unlike those of ancestors within a family, the memories of these structures are a reminder of our past and provide a connection to our future.

The People's House

On December 30, 1868, the Alabama legislature approved the establishment of a new county from land obtained from Autauga, Bibb, Shelby and Perry Counties. Named for Alfred Baker, the new section was established, in part, because of the rapid population growth in central Alabama. The inconvenience of traveling to a distant county seat to conduct business convinced residents that they would be better served by a more convenient center of local government.

The first courthouse to serve Baker County was established in the settlement of Grantville. Constructed by A.J. Cooper for the sum of $5,000, the building was a one-room log structure described as appearing more like a kitchen than a courthouse. A judge of the Second Judicial Circuit held court in the new building on the first Monday in March and September.

In 1870, the courthouse was destroyed by fire, an event that would have a significant impact on the future of Grantville and Baker County. On the first Saturday of April 1871, a referendum was held to determine the location of a new courthouse. The towns of Benson (Isabella), Clanton (formerly Goose Pond), Lomax and Verbena were proposed as the new seat of county government. Because no town received a majority in the initial voting, a second election was held. After the ballots were counted, Clanton became the new county seat.

A special tax was levied to raise funds for construction of a new courthouse and jail. Erected in 1872 and located at what is now the intersection of Second Avenue North and Sixth Street, the new courthouse was a two-story frame building that was considered a fine and expensive structure.

On December 17, 1874, in response to a petition by residents, the legislature approved a measure to rename Baker County for William Parish Chilton, former chief justice of the Alabama Supreme Court. Consequently, the Baker County Courthouse became the Chilton County Courthouse.

By 1894, the first courthouse in Clanton no longer provided adequate space to accommodate the increasing numbers of citizens attending the spring and fall terms of the court. After considerable debate, commissioners approved construction of a new courthouse. Completed in 1896, the brick structure was located on the corner of Second Avenue North and Sixth Street only a short distance from its predecessor.

In 1918, a fire of unknown origin severely damaged the interior of the building. Delos Hughes, author of *Historic Alabama Courthouses*, relates that a grand jury charged to investigate the fire did not report that arson was involved. Because the exterior walls of the structure remained standing, commissioners initiated a project to rebuild and modernize the courthouse. The project included the addition of a new front section to the 1896 building. This new addition consisted of steps leading to a massive portico supported by four Ionic-style columns.

The $60,000 cost of the reconstruction project created such a severe threat to the financial future of the county that the commissioner's court canceled all farm demonstration services and road maintenance programs. Ultimately, the cost proved to be justified, as the *Union Banner* described the transformation as "rising majestically from the ashes of the former courthouse, the new structure is one of the most beautiful county buildings in Alabama." In October 1919, the first session of the commissioner's court was convened in the building that would serve as the seat of Chilton County government for more than four decades.

The fourth Chilton County courthouse would serve as the seat of county government and gathering place for residents for more than forty years.

More than just an administration building, the courthouse served as a gathering place for local officials, retirees and residents having an interest in county government. Most afternoons, people would gather on the steps of the courthouse to discuss current issues, swap stories and hear the latest gossip.

By 1954, the structural integrity of the fourth seat of county government had deteriorated significantly. After an inspection, the state fire marshal reported that the structure had served well beyond the economic and efficient life of such a building in a growing and progressive county.

Following six years of discussion and debate, a referendum was held in February 1960 to allow the citizens to determine whether a new courthouse should be constructed. The ballot also included the question of where to locate the new structure. Voters overwhelmingly approved construction of a new courthouse building to be located on the same site.

Prior to beginning construction, the Chilton County Board of Revenue and Control purchased a parcel of property that adjoined the courthouse property. The new building was erected to the east of its predecessor on the recently acquired parcel of land and a parking lot installed where the former courthouse stood. On February 18, 1962, Governor John Patterson attended the ceremony dedicating the new facility.

When progress and local customs collide, compromise is often the solution. The front steps of the new courthouse proved less accommodating for the informal conduct of business and the traditional afternoon gatherings of retirees. The simple solution to a seemingly complex problem was construction of what became known as the Old Folks Shed, an open-sided aluminum structure built to create a shaded area like that previously provided by the portico of the old courthouse. Appropriately, the Old Folks Shed was constructed only a few feet from where the front steps of the previous courthouse building had served a similar purpose for more than four decades.

Five buildings have served as the center of county government during the 150-year history of Chilton County. Although the buildings may change, the presence of the People's House continuously reaffirms the words of Abraham Lincoln that "government of the people, by the people, for the people, shall not perish from the Earth."

A Daily Reminder

In cities across America, certain prominent buildings define the downtown districts. With the passage of generations, these structures and the memories associated with them become an important part of the identity and history of a community. In Clanton, two prominent and historic structures, the First Baptist Church and First United Methodist Church, have maintained an enduring presence in the city, serving for generations as foundations of stability and beacons of hope in an often turbulent and rapidly changing world.

The memberships of the Baptist and Methodist churches were organized shortly after the founding of the city of Clanton. Prior to the first church buildings being erected, congregations would gather in any available location. The Methodists initially met in a one-room school building located on the corner of Second Avenue North and Third Street. Similarly, *The History of the First Baptist Church, 1872–1983* relates, "The seeds from which has grown the Baptist Church were sown by pioneer preachers in schoolhouses, vacant stores and in the Courthouse."

During 1872–73, Alfred Baker, a Protestant Methodist minister and founder of Clanton, donated small parcels of land to the congregations of both denominations to construct permanent houses of worship. The Baptists built a single-story wood-frame building on the corner of Second Avenue North and Fourth Street. For construction of their new church, the Methodists were given a parcel of land located on Eighth Street that overlooked downtown. Until construction of their small, one-story white frame building was completed, the group met under a tent erected on the site.

Left: Completed in 1921, the First Baptist Church has been a prominent and historic landmark in downtown Clanton for more than one hundred years.

Below: The Clanton First United Methodist Church has occupied the same parcel of land since 1872 and is the third building to serve its congregation.

Attendance at religious services during the period required a sense of dedication and endurance. During the summer months, open windows and palmetto fans provided the only means of relief from the heat. With the arrival of winter, pot-bellied stoves were stoked throughout the service to keep worshippers warm. The cleansing waters of Goose Pond Creek were used by the Baptist church for baptisms of those who professed their faith.

In May 1888, the congregation of the Methodist church dedicated a new church building located on the same site as their first house of worship. The new building was adorned with a steeple and bell tower. In January 1890, a committee from the Baptist church approved construction of a new sanctuary to be built on land donated by Dr. J.S. Johnson that was located on the corner of Second Avenue North and Sixth Street.

These pillars of the community were again transformed beginning in February 1920 when the Baptist congregation approved construction of a new church building. Completed in November 1921, the massive all-brick structure has been a principal landmark in downtown Clanton for more than one hundred years.

Two years later, in November 1923, the cornerstone of a new Methodist church building was carefully placed on the same hallowed ground that the congregation had occupied for fifty years. Throughout their histories, both churches would continue to expand their ministries to reach those in need, both in and beyond the city that has been their home for 150 years.

The houses of worship that are the First Baptist Church and First United Methodist Church have served the city of Clanton as foundations of stability and beacons of hope through the passing of a century. Facing east, the stained-glass windows of the Methodist church are touched by the golden rays of the morning sun while those of the Baptist church, facing west, are bathed in the softening glow of the setting sun, a daily reminder of the words of Psalm 113:3, "From the rising of the sun to its setting, the name of the Lord is to be praised."

A Thing of Great Beauty

On a beautiful Sunday morning in August 1926, a congregation of more than three hundred people gathered for the morning worship service in the new sanctuary of the Clanton Methodist Church. An article in the *Union Banner* described the service as consisting of special music performed by the choir and a thoughtful and impressive sermon appropriate to the usages of the new building provided by Pastor C.C. Wilkerson. Because construction had been ongoing for three or four years, the *Union Banner* article emphasized that the new building spoke volumes for those who made its existence possible.

Perhaps the most impressive features of the new sanctuary were the two large murals and elaborate artwork that surrounded the chancel and choir loft. Created by artist C.V. Malmede, these beautiful works of art have continued to inspire and encourage generations of worshippers for almost one hundred years.

Born in the Federal Republic of Germany in 1864, Clovis Valentine Malmede moved with his family to Belgium, where his father established the International Commercial College. As a young man, Malmede immigrated to the United States, first making his home in Vermont. After relocating to Ohio, where he became a naturalized citizen, Malmede pursued his artistic passion to become an interior designer and decorator who specialized in refurbishing churches, mausoleums, and theaters.

Following the death of his wife, Malmede married the former Belle Johnston Matthews of Clanton in September 1920 in Lima, Ohio. In 1923, Malmede accepted a position with the Boys Industrial School in Birmingham, where he organized courses in art.

A former member of the Clanton Methodist Church, Belle Matthews Malmede persuaded her husband that a thing of great beauty should adorn the interior of the new sanctuary. In *A History of the Clanton First United Methodist Church*, local historian Helen Parrish writes, "The painting of the murals was accomplished during the coldest part of the winter and took three months to complete." Each day, as Malmede ascended the scaffold to begin painting, a group of local children would congregate nearby, sitting on the floor, watching intently as the artist brought stories from the Bible to life.

These inspiring works of art depict two scenes from the Book of John: Jesus and the woman at the well, as described in John 4:1–30, and Christ and Mary Magdalene at the empty tomb, from the words of John 20:1–18. The artist dedicated both works in honor of his wife, Belle Matthews Malmede.

According to Helen Parrish, the only expense for this work consisted of supplies and the cost of room and board for Malmede at the nearby Wilson Hotel.

The patron of these works of art, Belle Matthews Malmede, died in January 1933 and was buried next to her first husband, Dr. Emmett Abram Matthews, in the Clanton Cemetery. C.V. Malmede would remain

Left: The Clanton First United Methodist Church mural depicting Jesus and the woman at the well.

Right: The mural of the Clanton First United Methodist Church depicting Mary Magdalene at the entrance of the empty tomb.

in Birmingham until his death in January 1942. He was laid to rest in the Forrest Hills Cemetery.

Today, almost one hundred years after being created by the colors and brushes of Clovis Valentine Malmede, the murals that have so beautifully conveyed the story of the life and resurrection of Jesus continue to provide a sense of comfort, inspiration and encouragement to all who gather in his name. As the morning sunlight transcends the stained-glass windows of the sanctuary, the soft, multicolored glow highlights these poignant reminders of the words for all of God's children found in Matthew 18:20, "For where two or three gather in my name, there am I with them."

Camp Clanchilala

In May 1935, during the worst economic decline in United States history, twenty-two young men arrived in Clanton to begin work clearing a twelve-acre parcel of land located one mile west of the city along the Selma Highway. The property was part of the Joe Mullins farm that had been leased to the federal government for the establishment of a camp to accommodate 250 young men from across the United States.

Personnel of the U.S. Army supervised construction of the facility. The barracks, mess hall and administration buildings were almost identical in appearance to a military post. Although not members of the armed forces, men assigned to the camp would serve in the Tree Army, a term used to describe thousands of workers across the nation laboring in public works projects initiated during the administration of President Franklin Roosevelt. These programs promoted environmental conservation and the development of good citizenship through vigorous, disciplined outdoor labor.

Camp Clanchilala, a name derived from the location of the camp (Clanton, Chilton, Alabama), was operated by the Civilian Conservation Corps. Established in 1933, the program was a component of the New Deal economic agenda created to reduce high rates of unemployment. Known locally as the CCC Camp, the facility was one of more than one hundred camps that operated within the state of Alabama from 1933 until 1942.

The primary mission of Camp Clanchilala was soil conservation. Workers constructed retention ponds, terraced farm fields and planted trees, grass and vines to control soil erosion. One of the most common methods used

The Civilian Conservation Corps operated Camp Clanchilala to accommodate workers assigned to soil conservation projects in Chilton County. *Thomas Horton Walker.*

to prevent erosion was sowing the topsoil with a new type of invasive vine known as kudzu.

The CCC program was terminated in 1942 with United States intervention in the Second World War. Domestic employment increased dramatically as manufacturers across the nation increased production to support the war effort. The history of Camp Clanchilala would not end with the economic recovery, however. Ironically, the facility created to fight the war against poverty would also serve in the battle against hostile aggression during the Second World War.

During the spring of 1943, following four years of bloody conflict in Europe, the United States and its allies achieved a decisive victory over German and Italian military forces in North Africa. The defeat proved disastrous for the Third Reich, with more than 350,000 members of its elite Afrika Korps estimated to have been killed or taken prisoner.

Captured enemy soldiers were initially detained in secure facilities in Great Britain. By the summer of 1943, however, the British were unable to accommodate increasing numbers of prisoners because of limited capacity within their detention facilities. To alleviate this problem, the United States agreed to accept fifty thousand prisoners of war. By 1945, that number had increased to more than four hundred thousand prisoners held in camps across the United States.

To provide the necessary accommodations for this influx of prisoners, the Army Corps of Engineers was tasked with the responsibility of constructing secure camps, primarily in the southeastern and southwestern United States. For security purposes, camps were situated on military bases or sites located significant distances from major cities and industrial centers.

Existing facilities such as those previously utilized by the Civilian Conservation Corps were frequently converted into makeshift prisoner of war camps. During 1943, more than twenty former Civilian Conservation Corps facilities in Alabama were converted into prisoner of war camps. Known as branch or satellite camps, these facilities provided additional capacity to support the four main prisoner of war camps in Alabama: Fort McClellan at Anniston, Fort Rucker at Ozark, Aliceville and Opelika.

Branch camps served an economic purpose as well. The migration of farm workers to metropolitan areas in search of industrial jobs created severe labor shortages in rural areas of the country that were heavily dependent on the agriculture and timber industries. From 1943–45, the prisoner of war population in branch camps in Alabama continued to increase to facilitate the use of prison labor in these industries.

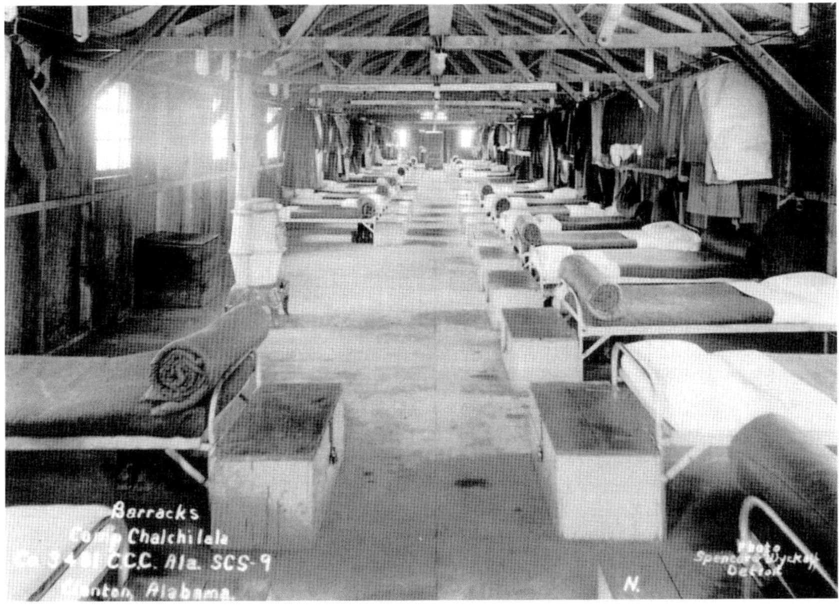

The barracks of Camp Clanchilala provided basic accommodations for workers. These barracks would house German prisoners during the Second World War. *Thomas Horton Walker.*

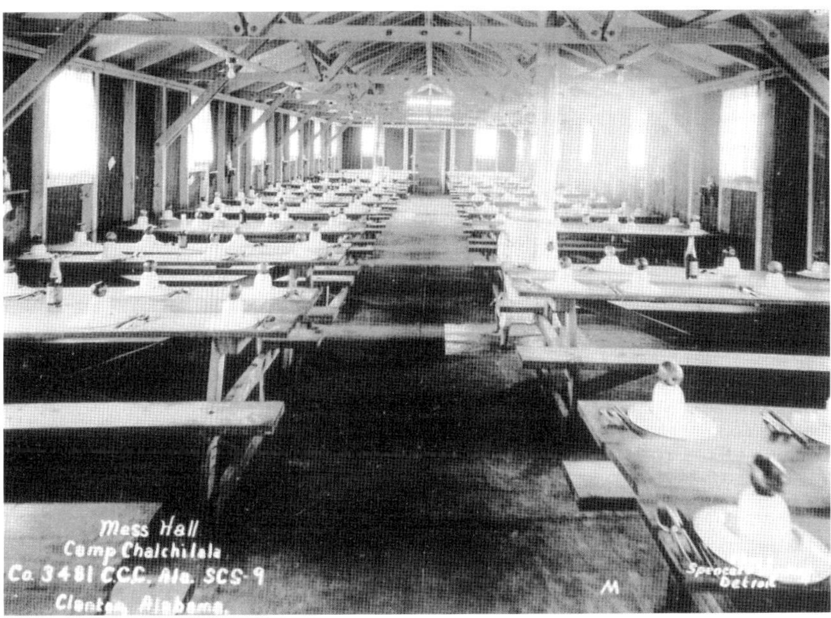

The mess hall of Camp Clanchilala provided daily meals for more than two hundred workers. *Thomas Horton Walker.*

In June 1944, the headline of an article in the *Union Banner* read, "War Prisoners Kept at Old CCC Camp Here," as the first contingent of German prisoners of war arrived in Clanton. A report by the office of the provost marshal described Camp Clanton as being situated "on landscaped grounds, with much green and shrubbery, well repaired and enlarged; the prison population of the camp working in the compound, sawmills and lumberyards and enjoying a small canteen with a day-room attached; two ping-pong tables, various games and movies twice each week as well as a library of eighty fiction and fifty other books."

For residents of Chilton County, the former Civilian Conservation Corps camp, operating as a satellite facility under the supervision of the prisoner of war camp at Fort McClellan, appeared more formidable with the addition of an electric perimeter fence reinforced with barbed wire. Guard towers were positioned at each corner of the post. During hours of darkness, large spotlights illuminated the facility and surrounding area. A veil of secrecy surrounded the operation of Camp Clanton, making it one of the most obscure and intriguing aspects of the history of Chilton County. During the Second World War, censorship of the news media for reasons of national security resulted in limited public knowledge about specific aspects of the war both at home and abroad. Information about Camp Clanton was so restricted that many residents of Chilton County were unaware of its existence.

By July 1945, 206 German prisoners of war were incarcerated at the camp. According to an article in the *Union Banner*, "The men could not be told from Americans except for their talking; they are of fine physique, perfectly proportioned, sound as a dollar and strong as an ox." Under the provisions of the United States War Manpower Commission, prisoners were available for employment in local businesses. Former German soldiers were hired to harvest timber and to work in sawmills and as laborers on local farms. The prisoners were paid prevailing rates for their labor but only allowed to keep eighty cents per day to purchase luxury items at the camp commissary. Armed guards provided constant supervision.

In Chilton County, the *Union Banner* reported that "prisoners will be used at various work jobs in the vicinity. It is said that some will cut pulpwood for Mr. Otto Jones, some will work on the farm of W.L. Parrish and some for Stapp's Dairy." German prisoners were transported to and from their work assignments on military trucks and would frequently wave to bystanders as they passed through Clanton.

As a young man growing up in Thorsby, Douglas Cleckler envisioned German soldiers as being sinister and evil, like those depicted in newsreel clips in theaters. According to Cleckler, "The Germans were supposed to be bad guys. We imagined them as monsters." Cleckler was surprised during his first encounter with German prisoners. He would often sit on the side of the highway near his home in Thorsby and watch the prisoners at work at the local lumber mill and was astounded to discover "they did not appear threatening. They were young men, most in their mid-twenties with the typical blond hair and blue eyes. One of the prisoners spoke fluent English."

Cleckler once asked the English-speaking prisoner if he regretted being captured. Without hesitation, the prisoner replied, "No son, I am here in America. I have a bed and three meals each day. When this war is over, I will be allowed to return to whatever remains of my home and family. I am one of the lucky ones. I was captured, not killed."

The first impression of Douglas Cleckler was common. Co-workers often found the Germans to be hardworking, personable and friendly. However, this impression would change for many residents following the June 1945 publication of a letter submitted to the editor of the *Union Banner* by a Chilton County soldier involved in the liberation of German concentration camps in Europe.

Clifford Morris Keen grew up in the Shiloh community near Clanton. During the Second World War, Sergeant Keen served in the Forty-Second Rainbow Infantry Division. Following the surrender of the German Wehrmacht, Keen and his fellow infantrymen were deployed to southern Germany to liberate the Nazi concentration camp at Dachau. In a graphic letter that described the atrocities that occurred in the camp, Keen wrote, "The crimes done behind the walls of this, the worst of Nazi concentration camps, now live only to haunt the memories of the soldiers who tore open its gates and first saw its misery."

The publication of Sergeant Keen's letter created an immediate local reaction. Many respondents compared the brutal treatment of American and other prisoners in Germany to the perceived comfort enjoyed by prisoners incarcerated in the United States. One subscriber explained the attitude of some residents in response to the German prisoners being transported on military vehicles through Clanton. "The Germans wave at us all; we stand and turn our backs to them. They are devils. We don't wave at trash."

Sergeant L.D. Williams of Clanton wrote, "American soldiers are often disciplined for fraternizing with the German people, but what about civilians back home fraternizing with German prisoners? I am referring to the movies, dances and good times enjoyed by the prisoners of war, including approximately $27 per month earned on jobs that is more than most of us got early in the war. We eat only rations while they fill their bellies on steaks and fresh vegetables."

After four years of living with rationing of food, gasoline and other necessities, one citizen complained, "I have gone to the ice plant for ice and there are trucks getting loads of ice for the Germans and I am turned down; they tell me they haven't got it, but they won't see the Germans turned down." Another subscriber wrote, "I don't tolerate that the Germans are given beer as Chilton is a dry county, and our own people aren't allowed to have it. I don't think it right for the Germans to be given things that we ourselves have to do without." Resentment of the German prisoners of war would be short-lived. In September 1945, following the end of the war in Europe, Camp Clanton was closed and the detainees repatriated to their home countries.

After the war, most of the military records relating to prisoner of war camps in the United States were destroyed, making it difficult to accurately re-create the history of individual facilities. In his book *The Fort McClellan POW Camp: German Prisoners in Alabama 1943–1946*, Jack Shay relates a personal account of one of the most remarkable episodes in the history of the Clanton prisoner of war camp that was never made public because of censorship of the news media during the war: the escape of two prisoners and their attempt to evade capture in Chilton County.

In September 1944, a group of German prisoners were transported from Fort McClellan to Clanton to work at a local lumber company. Within days of their incarceration, the commanding officer of Camp Clanton received a late-night call from Chilton County sheriff J. Alvin Nivens, who advised that he had two German prisoners of war in his custody at the Chilton County Jail.

During the subsequent interrogation, the prisoners confessed that they had received word that Adolf Hitler, chancellor of the German Reich, planned to send a naval transport to Argentina in February 1945 to provide passage for escaped prisoners of war to return to Germany. The two prisoners had devised a plan of escape soon after their arrival in Clanton. During a distraction created by a group of fellow prisoners, the two men slipped into the woods. At roll call, other prisoners would answer in their place so their absence would not be noticed.

The night of their escape, however, the men were caught in a severe thunderstorm that produced heavy rain and hail. Seeking refuge, the prisoners made their way to the porch of an old farmhouse. Seeing no lights illuminated, the men thought the house was empty. Asleep inside the house, the occupants were startled awake by voices coming from the porch. The farmer arose, grabbed his shotgun and confronted the escapees.

Because the Germans did not speak English, they were unable to explain their presence on the property. Having no telephone, the farmer immediately sent his wife to the house of a neighbor to call the sheriff. Arriving at the scene, Sheriff Nivens immediately handcuffed the prisoners. Searching for weapons, the sheriff discovered homemade knives with wooden handles, which had been crafted in the wood shop of the camp, secured to the leg of each prisoner. Routine searches at Camp Clanton had not revealed the knives prior to the escape attempt. The prisoners were returned to Fort McClellan and punished with the standard two weeks of solitary confinement.

Camp Clanton represents one of the many contributions of Chilton County in the effort to defeat the Axis powers during the Second World War. Although the passing of more than seventy years has consigned the story of Camp Clanton to a footnote in the annals of military history, it remains one of the most significant and unique aspects of the history of Chilton County.

The Columns on First Street

During the predawn darkness of a chilly Tuesday morning in November 1938, Mrs. Jimmie Taylor was awakened suddenly by the sound of breaking glass. Peering nervously through the front window of her home to identify the source of the noise, Taylor was horrified to observe a raging fire engulfing the Chilton County High School building across the street.

Although the Clanton Volunteer Fire Department answered the call immediately, the conflagration was well underway by the time they arrived. According to the *Union Banner*, attempts to quell the blaze were hampered by a shortage of water and a broken pressure valve on the fire truck.

Constructed in 1914, the two-story brick building was situated on a twenty-acre parcel of land located at the corner of First Street and Second Avenue South. Initially, the location of the county high school had been the subject of local debate. The issue was resolved when the state board of education made the decision to locate the school in the county seat of Clanton as opposed to an alternate site in Jemison.

Ironically, the same edition of the *Union Banner* that informed readers of the destruction of the school also included a feature article, "Fire Hazard in Schools Brings State Warning." The article quotes the superintendent of

Opened in September 1940, the school on First Street would serve the educational needs of the community for more than six decades.

education warning, "It is essential that every precaution be taken to prevent fire loss in school buildings."

The board of education approved the issuance of bonds to construct a new building on the original site on First Street. During construction, 390 displaced students attended classes in an annex of the Clanton First Baptist Church and other schools in the county.

Opened to students in September 1940, the new Chilton County High School consisted of eighteen classrooms, sanitary bathrooms, a laboratory, a gymnasium and a library; it was a facility described as being modern in every respect. In December 1947, seven years after the new school building was completed, a second fire destroyed the gymnasium and most of the classrooms in the south wing of the building. The section damaged by the fire was rebuilt the following year.

By 1962, increasing student enrollment required the construction of a larger high school facility. Located on Seventh Avenue South, the new Chilton County High School opened to students at the beginning of the 1962–63 school year. The buildings of the former high school would continue

The former school was demolished in March 2006; its columns were left standing as a tribute to past students and teachers.

to serve the educational needs of students for more than four decades, first as a junior high school and subsequently as a middle school. The middle school was more commonly known as Adair, named for the respected educator Henry M. Adair.

In March 2006, having served as an institution of learning for more than six decades, the buildings that were once the Chilton County High School were again destroyed, not by fire or natural disaster but to accommodate the demands of a growing education system.

For the first time in almost a century, the corner of First Street and Second Avenue South stood bare; the massive columns that once adorned the entrance of this proud facility were left standing as a final tribute to generations of students and faculty members who passed through its doors. Even though the physical structure has been relegated to history, memories of the school will be forever ingrained in the hearts of those who shared its legacy.

The Tuskegee Hangar

During the Second World War, the state of Alabama served a crucial role in the evolution of military airpower as the foundation of the great arsenal of democracy envisioned by President Franklin Roosevelt. For the five-year period 1941–45, more than sixty thousand military aviators were trained at bases located in Montgomery, Selma, Dothan, Courtland and Foley.

Perhaps the most notable military aviation training base in Alabama during the Second World War was the Tuskegee Army Air Field. Activated in August 1941, the Tuskegee Army Air Field was the only facility in the United States established to provide military flight training for African American cadets.

Located seven miles northwest of the town of Tuskegee, the air base consisted of 1,680 acres of land that included four paved runways and more than 225 buildings to accommodate the military and civilian personnel assigned to the installation. The training aircraft based at the field were maintained in three large hangars of steel construction.

Before being deactivated in June 1947, approximately one thousand aviation cadets graduated from the flight training programs at Tuskegee.

One of three hangars originally located at the Tuskegee Army Air Field, this structure was relocated in 1948 to the Chilton County Airport.

These men became known as the Tuskegee Airmen, the first African Americans to serve as pilots in the armed forces of the United States. Following the end of the war, the buildings and structures located on the Tuskegee Army Air Field and other bases were declared surplus and assigned to the War Assets Administration for disposal.

In January 1948, an article in the *Union Banner* quoted Probate judge W.L. Parrish stating, "Chilton County has secured a large airplane hangar from the Tuskegee Army Air Base." It was obtained through an "as is, where is" agreement, and the commissioners court approved an allocation of $10,000 dollars to disassemble, transport and erect the newly acquired hangar on the Chilton County Airport.

The new hangar had an immediate impact on residents of Chilton County. In addition to its primary use as a storage facility for aircraft, the hangar was also utilized as a venue for numerous community events. Soon after being erected, the hangar became the focal point of the 1948 peach festival. Activities that included the peach judging, peach auction and a gospel concert were held inside the historic structure. Because of the large amount of floor space, the hangar was also a popular location for livestock shows, agricultural exhibits and dances.

For many residents, the most memorable event associated with the hangar occurred during the 1954 peach festival. As the closing event, the Blackwood Brothers gospel quartet was scheduled to perform from a stage erected at the west end of the hangar. Only minutes before their performance, quartet members R.W. Blackwood and Bill Lyles were fatally injured in an aircraft accident at the airport. Johnny Ogburn, the son of Thorsby civic leader Archie Ogburn, also perished in the crash.

Five weeks later, the reorganized Blackwood Brothers Quartet returned to Clanton for a memorial concert in the hangar. More than five thousand people attended the event.

The passing of eight decades has taken its toll on the Tuskegee hangar. Although some of its original components have been replaced or reinforced, the building continues to serve in its original capacity, protecting airplanes from the harsh effects of the sun, wind and rain. More than a storage facility, however, the Tuskegee hangar stands as a symbol of a remarkable period in the history of both the United States and Chilton County.

The Clanton Drive-In

In October 1949, a new Saturday night ritual in Chilton County commenced with the grand opening of the Clanton Drive-In Theatre. Vehicles filled with teenagers began passing through the two-lane ticket booth of the outdoor cinema in a rite of passage that would be handed down to their children and, in some cases, their grandchildren.

Located three miles north of Clanton on Highway 31, the facility was described in a *Union Banner* article as the most beautiful drive-in theater in the Southland, consisting of fifteen acres of land converted into a veritable fairyland of flowers and shrubs.

Owner Joseph Able Jackson designed the Clanton drive-in to not only accommodate cars; he also included special ramps for trucks. In the *Union Banner* article, Jackson stressed that "every farmer for miles around who wants to load his family and neighbors onto a truck to enjoy a movie at the drive-in will be as welcome as the flowers in May."

In summertime, should the interior of the vehicle become too warm for comfort, bleachers that would easily seat three hundred people were positioned directly in front of the huge projection screen. A large speaker was installed adjacent to the bleachers to provide sound for the movie. For parents in need of an evening of relaxation, a playground that included swings, a sliding board and sandboxes was situated near the bleachers to occupy the attention of their young children.

Features included top-flight movies being shown almost as soon as they were introduced to audiences in New York and other major metropolitan areas. Newsreels, comedies and short subjects were provided to supplement feature presentations.

Although it was advertised as a family entertainment venue, Saturday nights at the drive-in belonged to high school juniors and seniors from Clanton and surrounding communities. As the sun set on Saturday afternoons, groups of teenagers would squeeze into automobiles and the beds of pickup trucks and onto motorcycles to compete for strategically located parking slots at the drive-in. Economies of scale could be achieved by hiding friends in the trunk of the car until past the admission gate.

Once inside, automobiles were positioned using a time-honored, strictly enforced tradition: Chilton County High School students situated in one corner, those from Jemison in another, with Thorsby, Verbena and Maplesville occupying prearranged locations in the middle.

Located on Highway 31, the Clanton Drive-In was described as the most beautiful theater in the Southland and remained in operation for more than thirty years.

An evening at the drive-in, while providing an ironclad alibi for parents, was less about enjoying the featured attraction than spending time socializing with friends, treating a date to an inexpensive dinner at the concession stand or resolving disputes between members of opposing high school sports teams. Most important, however, the Clanton drive-in afforded a safe haven for first dates. If the attraction between a young couple on their first date proved to be mutual, an evening in front of the big screen provided a modicum of privacy. If chemistry between the two failed to materialize, the ever-present group of friends nearby served as a convenient safety net.

By 1982, competition from the local Mart Twin Theaters, offering multiple features in air-conditioned comfort, ended the Saturday night ritual of dinner and a movie at the drive-in. Today, the abandoned site of the Clanton Drive-In Theatre serves as a poignant reminder of a simpler time when teens routinely interacted without the benefit of Snapchat, FaceTime or Messenger.

The Tourist Court

In the fall of 1926, Chilton County entered a new era of economic opportunity and prosperity. The dirt surface of the Birmingham to Montgomery Highway had recently been improved with an overlay of concrete, allowing for faster, more reliable travel along the route. The highway became part of the Dixie Bee Line, an all-paved, 1,035-mile route connecting the cities of Miami and Chicago. The Dixie Bee Line was designed to accommodate a new generation of travelers who preferred the personal freedom of the automobile to the restrictive scheduling of the railroad.

Prior to 1930, individuals utilizing automobiles for transportation across long distances were known as "tin can tourists" because they literally lived in their vehicles while traveling to their destination, filling their automobile with enough canned food to last for the duration of their trip. Because they often set up camps along the road to spend the night, these energetic travelers were described as traveling with one shirt and a twenty-dollar bill and never changing either.

Recognizing a new economic opportunity, entrepreneurs began constructing small tourist camps along these major thoroughfares. Typically, these sites furnished several amenities for the weary traveler that included heat in the winter, electric fans in the summer and private baths. These modern facilities were known as tourist courts.

Unlike early hotels that catered to railroad passengers, tourist courts offered small stand-alone cottages that looked and functioned like small homes. These tourist courts provided convenient access to the highway and were designed so that automobiles could be conveniently parked in front of the cottage.

Located at the midpoint between Birmingham and Montgomery, Clanton became an oasis of tourist courts. One such facility, Ike's Motor Court and Café, was located on Highway 31 two miles north of Clanton. Owned and operated by Ike Bice, the modern all-brick buildings were guaranteed to be 100 percent fireproof. Each room had fully carpeted floors, tile baths and circulating ice water. Guests could dine in the café while having their automobiles serviced on-site.

Equipped with the modern convenience of air-conditioning, the Ellis Tourist Court was advertised as the "Best Stop Between Key West and the North Pole." Conveniently located on Highway 31 in Clanton, the Ellis Tourist Court also enticed guests by advertising the availability of heavenly sleep on comfortable Beautyrest mattresses.

The Ellis Tourist Court, located on the Birmingham to Montgomery Highway, was advertised as the best stop between Key West and the North Pole.

Located one mile south of Clanton, the Cloverleaf Motel introduced a new concept in overnight lodging. The owners, Mr. and Mrs. Roscoe Williams, referred to their establishment as a motel instead of a tourist court. A combination of the words motor and hotel, the term implied increased comfort and convenience, even though motels and tourist courts were similar in appearance and amenities provided. Over the years, guests at the Cloverleaf Motel would continue to enjoy relaxing luxuries that included a television in each room and a modern swimming pool.

Construction of Interstate 65 through Chilton County marked the beginning of the end for tourist courts in Clanton and elsewhere. Along the interstate, seemingly identical hotels with names like Holiday Inn and Ramada Inn soon replaced the unique character of hometown tourist courts. In a sense, history is repeating itself, as interstate travelers today have become "paper bag tourists," spending time stuck in traffic eating fast food out of a paper bag and only taking time for a brief nap at one of the roadside camps now known as hotels.

A Bold, Beautiful Spring

In December 1889, the *Clanton View* included the announcement, "Last week, Captain W. A. Smith of Dixie purchased the Mineral Springs property. There on the property is a bold, beautiful spring, strongly impregnated with mineral water gushing out of the white pebbles." The article concluded, "The new owners have ample means and intend to erect a commodious hotel and otherwise improve what they believe to be valuable property. The large hotel is to be utilized as a health resort and will be finished by summer."

The resort and adjoining property were purchased in 1905 by physicians J.M. Robinson and R.B. McNeil. In addition to the hotel, the new owners erected cabins to accommodate guests. The new health resort became a prominent recreation and vacation spot for people from all sections of Alabama and nearby states. Visitors arrived by horse, by wagon and from the Louisville and Nashville Railroad depot at Jemison to partake of the restorative powers of the water.

A stairway provided access from the hotel to the gazebo that covered the bold, beautiful spring that produced healing waters at the Mineral Springs resort. *Glenn Littleton.*

Situated on top of a hill, the forty-room hotel afforded a panoramic view of the pine forests surrounding the retreat. Guests could take advantage of the therapeutic natural springs by descending a series of wooden steps that led to a small gazebo where they could relax and enjoy the quiet solitude of nature or the company of friends.

By 1930, the effects of a national economic depression resulted in a decline in the number of guests visiting the resort. Eventually, the hotel was torn down and the materials sold and utilized for construction of private homes, barns and other structures.

In 1938, the deteriorating facility was purchased by renowned herb doctor Andrew Marshall Price. The *Union Banner* informed readers that "under the ownership of Dr. Price, The Springs have undergone considerable improvement and development. A forty-room hospital has been constructed and electricity has been brought in by the Alabama Power Company."

Known as the Mineral Springs Sanatorium, the facility included a hospital building with a combined café and drugstore. The hospital was located beside a wooded hill overlooking two large artificial lakes. In his office, Dr. Price would diagnose the diseases of patients and prescribe herbal remedies. The facility also offered hot and cold baths and a steam room and spa using water drawn from the springs. The staff of the sanatorium allowed residents of Clanton and surrounding communities to fill containers with the invigorating water of the springs at no cost.

The history of the Mineral Springs Sanatorium came to a tragic end on a frigid night in December 1949 as two young men from Birmingham robbed the hospital. Giving chase in his car, Dr. Price caught the culprits on a road near Union Grove. During the ensuing confrontation, Price was shot by one of the offenders and succumbed to his wounds.

Following the death of Dr. Price, ownership of the property passed among different groups that included the Mineral Springs Backwoods Village and Gardens, the King's Ranch and the Alabama Department of Youth Services. According to a history published in *The Heritage of Chilton County*, legendary football coach Paul "Bear" Bryant was once an owner of the property.

Today, nature has reclaimed much of what remains of the popular resort and sanatorium. In the calm of early evening, however, the faint sound of the bold, beautiful spring transcends history as the sparkling water comes gushing out among the white pebbles.

Turn Around, Chilton County's Natural Showplace

In August 1874, newly appointed state geologist Eugene Allen Smith set out from Prattville in a mule-drawn wagon to conduct a geological survey of central Alabama. The purpose of the survey, mandated by the Alabama legislature, was to identify natural resources that could be used to develop industry in the state. Industrial development was critical to rebuilding the state economy in the aftermath of the American Civil War.

Entering Chilton County near Verbena, Smith initially followed a course that paralleled the Louisville and Nashville Railroad. From the Verbena station, the geologist detoured approximately three miles to the east along Chestnut Creek to an area known as Turn Around.

In his *Geological Survey of Alabama, Report of Progress for 1874*, Smith described Turn Around as "the point where the creek is deflected from its course by a high ridge. After making a circuit of the ridge, of a mile or more, it returns on the other side; the two parts of the creek separated by this high ridge being only about fifty yards apart." A person standing at a certain point on the ridge could observe sections of the creek flowing in each of the four cardinal directions of the compass.

In September 1898, Smith returned to Turn Around and climbed to the top of what he identified as Turn Around Rock. Smith described this unusual formation as consisting of hard, erosion-resistant rock rising from a steep, narrow ridge that plunged sharply down to Chestnut Creek. He theorized that softer stone beneath the arch cap had eroded over thousands of years to form the opening.

In time, the geological survey completed by Eugene Smith did benefit the state of Alabama and Chilton County. In 1908, the Flaketown Graphite Company established a mine approximately two miles east of Verbena to extract graphite for distribution to customers throughout the United States.

The land holdings of the Flaketown Graphite Company included the area known as Turn Around. In *Chilton County and Her People*, T.E. Wyatt noted that Edmond R. Taber, owner of the Flaketown Graphite Company, designed and developed scenic trails through the natural showplace of Chilton County. The trails extended for two miles along jagged cliffs lush with longleaf pines, azalea, dogwood and mountain laurel. During and immediately following the First World War, Taber and his sons installed hundreds of concrete steps along the winding trails to aid hikers in climbing and descending the steep terrain.

The stone columns at Turn Around remain standing more than seventy-five years after the last visitor passed through the gate.

By 1925, the Flaketown Graphite Company had terminated its mining operations. The landholdings were subsequently sold to the Alabama Machinery and Supply Company of Montgomery. Recognizing the scenic beauty of the area, the owners decided to develop the area as a public attraction.

An article in the April 1947 *Union Banner* informed readers that several thousand dollars had been spent at Turn Around during the past year to make

The remnants of concrete stairs that once were part of a two-mile trail that traversed the jagged cliffs and winding trails of Turn Around.

it one of central Alabama's showplaces. Workers installed handrails to make the trails safer for visitors making their way to picnic spots established along the ridgeline. Mr. and Mrs. J.W. Pitts, formerly of Montgomery, became the resident caretakers of Turn Around.

Out-of-town guests were directed to the park by a large sign located on Highway 31 south of Verbena. Visitors were charged an admission fee to spend a relaxing afternoon enjoying the scenic surroundings. A large parking area and concession stand were added at the entrance to accommodate visitors to the park.

The park at Turn Around operated for only a few years. As the gates closed for the final time, nature began the slow and tranquil process of reclaiming the land. Today, the passing of seven decades has hidden all but a few remnants of the attempts of man to improve on what nature first created. Left alone to take its course, nature will ensure that Turn Around is and forever remains the showplace of Chilton County.

The Thorsby Institute Bell

Established in September 1906, Thorsby Institute was envisioned as a preparatory school built on the foundation of nondenominational Christian principles. The inaugural catalogue advised, "The school is for young men and women of good minds and high aims who have conceived a serious purpose in life." However, the catalogue included a stern warning: "Vicious or idle boys not wanted." A high degree of scholarship, character and experience was demanded of every member of the faculty. Students received instruction in literature, music, theater, mathematics, history and foreign languages. As enrollment increased, Thorsby Institute became the first accredited high school in Chilton County.

BATES HALL AND CAMPUS

Thorsby Institute, Thorsby, Ala., is a Christian School of High Standard Where Expenses are Low.

Thorsby Institute was founded on Christian but nonsectarian principles and became the first accredited high school in Chilton County.

Bates Hall, named for the Reverend George Bates, pastor of the Pilgrim Congregational Church of Birmingham, was the largest structure on the Thorsby Institute campus. The two-story wood-frame building was adorned with a turret that contained the bell used to call students to class, chapel and other campus activities.

On April 27, 1925, the stillness of the late evening in Thorsby was broken by the sharp blasts of the whistle of the Louisville and Nashville Railroad's Pan American passenger train. Approaching the depot, the locomotive engineer realized that Bates Hall was aflame and used the whistle to alert the sleeping residents. According to the *Union Banner*, "The citizens of Thorsby did a valiant effort as volunteer firemen and used wet blankets on the roofs of adjacent buildings to keep the fire contained to Bates Hall." Tragically, the structure and all fixtures, including the bell, were destroyed.

Although a modern, all-brick building would be erected to replace Bates Hall, the small endowments received by Thorsby Institute were not sufficient to purchase a new bell. In the meantime, the school made use of a bell in a church located more than a block from campus.

In 1950, the Reverend Alva Hart, an instructor at Thorsby Institute, read a newspaper article about a railroad company that provided churches and other organizations with bells from steam locomotives being retired

Following a 1925 fire that destroyed the original Thorsby Institute bell, a replacement was obtained from the Chicago and Eastern Illinois Railroad.

from service. Reverend Hart contacted the president of the Chicago and Eastern Illinois Railroad in an effort to obtain a replacement bell for Thorsby Institute.

Within a week, a highly polished bell was secured in a crate and placed on a boxcar for shipment to Thorsby. The bell had previously been attached to a 1912 Brooks N-1 Class Mikado locomotive that pulled railcars of passengers and coal between Chicago and Evansville, Indiana. Ironically, the bell from the Chicago and Eastern Illinois Railroad arrived at the depot in Thorsby on a boxcar of the Louisville and Nashville Railroad. According to the Thorsby section of the *Union Banner*, "Although the bell has not yet been placed, we will soon hear it each morning at eight o'clock."

By 1957, however, financial difficulties forced the Thorsby Institute Board of Trustees to request a state grant to operate the school within the Chilton County school system for a period of two years. In 1959, the land and buildings of Thorsby Institute were deeded to the state of Alabama to be used as a high school.

Today, the Thorsby Institute Bell is displayed adjacent to the entrance of the Thorsby School, only a short distance from the original site of Bates Hall. Often, just before eight o'clock on mornings before classes begin, history repeats itself as the temptation becomes too great and a passing student sneaks a quick ring of the bell to start the new school day.

The Chilton County Training School, A Beacon of Inspiration

Educator Claire Fagin, the first woman to serve as president of an Ivy League university, once wrote, "Education creates the opportunity to make a difference." In 1924, the opportunity to make a difference for many young men and women of Chilton County was created on a five-acre parcel of land located five miles west of Clanton.

Conceived with the assistance of the Julius Rosenwald Fund, the Chilton County Training School became the first facility to provide minority students of Chilton County with the means to obtain a secondary education. The Julius Rosenwald Fund, established by the president of Sears, Roebuck and Company, provided the financial assistance needed to construct schools for African American students throughout the southeastern United States.

An important aspect of the Rosenwald Fund involved community participation in the construction of school projects. Residents were required to demonstrate their desire for a school by providing a suitable parcel of land for the facility and to contribute a percentage of the construction costs. To meet this requirement, land for the Chilton County Training School was donated by resident Ben Brown, while members of the community hosted fish fries and chicken dinners to raise the required matching funds. Building materials purchased in Maplesville were transported to the construction site by wagons owned by local families.

Completed in 1924 at a cost of approximately $5,000, the wood-frame building initially consisted of only five classrooms. In 1927, three additional classrooms were added to accommodate an equivalent increase in the number of teachers. The Chilton County Training School was one of more than four hundred education buildings in Alabama financed in part by the Rosenwald Fund. Students received not only instruction in academics but training in basic vocational and homemaking skills as well.

During the early years of the school, many students were able to attend classes only after completing their responsibilities at home or on the farm. Those who lived nearby walked to school, while students from Clanton and Lomax were transported on a bus operated by Ralph Odum. As enrollment continued to increase, the board of education eventually provided additional buses to transport students to and from communities throughout Chilton County.

To purchase supplies and support other educational needs, fundraising activities were sponsored by parents, teachers and students throughout the school year. Popular events included the annual harvest festival hosted by the parent-teacher association. During the festival, local farmers would be invited to display their produce to be judged for prizes and sold in a country fair setting. Another popular event, the May Day celebration, was held on the final day of school and included the traditional draping of the maypole in the blue-and-white school colors.

In December 1949, the main school building was destroyed by fire. For the next two years, classes were held in the vocational and home economics

Established in 1924, the Chilton County Training School provided secondary education for African American students from Clanton, Jemison, New Convert and Verbena.

buildings and other makeshift classrooms. In 1951, a new all-brick school building was completed, the first to include indoor plumbing.

A significant milestone in the history of the school was achieved in 1954 when the school received accreditation from the State of Alabama. This allowed graduates the opportunity to apply to colleges and universities without undue academic restrictions.

In subsequent years, a gymnasium, a science building and vocational, agricultural and home economics classrooms were constructed on an additional five acres of land purchased by the Chilton County Board of Education. For recreation, students could participate in organized sports such as volleyball, basketball, baseball and football. Nonathletic activities included various clubs and organizations, or students could advance their musical talents by joining the school band.

In 1969, after forty-five years of providing educational opportunities for minority students, the Chilton County Training School closed because of desegregation of the school system mandated by the 1964 Federal Civil Rights Act. The educational experiences provided by the Chilton County Training School created opportunities for graduates to make a difference in their local communities. A member of the class of 1963, Eddie Reed became the first minority to serve in public office in Chilton County when he was elected to the Jemison City Council. A career educator, Reed also served on the Chilton County Board of Education for ten years before being elected mayor of Jemison. In August 2020, he was elected to a fourth term in office. Another distinguished graduate, Bobby Agee, became the first minority member of the Chilton County Commission. Agee served with honor and distinction as a county commissioner for more than twenty years.

A lone brick chimney is one of the last remnants of the Chilton County Training School.

In 2007, the land and buildings of the former school were listed in the Alabama Register of Landmarks and History. Three years later, the Chilton County Training School Preservation Association was granted ownership of the property as part of an effort to preserve the site to inspire and encourage future generations. The Chilton County Training School was known to students as "the school on the hill," and its legacy continues to serve as a beacon of inspiration to those seeking an education to create the opportunity to make a difference.

Chapter 4

Solemn Memories

The history of a community is often engraved in the headstones of local cemeteries. The stories of those who came before us provide a sense of continuity through the passage of time. Even though the stories of our ancestors may be filled with sadness and tragedy, they often provide a sense of inspiration and hope for those who follow.

An Act of Compassion

Nestled among the once-majestic oak trees atop the crest of a small hill near the Jumbo community, the Williams-Goodgame Cemetery is the final resting place of Thomas H. Williams, the first sheriff to serve the people of Baker and, thereafter, Chilton County. To one side of this pioneer lawman are the remnants of an elaborate wrought-iron fence that once encircled the consecrated ground where the mortal remains of the Williams family were returned to the earth as described in the book of Genesis: "For dust thou art, and unto dust thou shalt return."

Strolling among the large ledger markers of the Williams family, it would be easy to overlook the small granite headstone that appears to be separated from the other graves yet seemingly occupies a special place unto itself. The one section of the old wrought-iron fence still standing, its condition reflective of the passing of more than a century, continues to protect this simple yet extraordinary marker.

This headstone relates the tragic story of an unknown child. The headstone is located in the Williams-Goodgame Cemetery in the Jumbo community.

Brushing away the accumulation of dirt and leaves from the small headstone reveals an inscription that tells a tragic story yet one that speaks of the genuine compassion of a stranger. Chiseled into the face of the marker are simple words that narrate the story of the brief life and death of a child whose name was known only to God and her parents. The inscription reads, "Unknown Girl, daughter of a family returning to SC from TX. She died from an illness as the family came through the Jumbo area and Sheriff Williams allowed her burial here. Died circa 1885."

Reading the obituary of the brief life of this unknown child in the peaceful calm of a late afternoon, the solitude broken only by the wind rustling the leaves of the trees, creates a sense of loss and sadness for the tragic passing of a life so long ago. The sound of a car on the road nearby arouses thoughts of the difficult journey from Texas to South Carolina that would have required months to complete by wagon, a trip that can easily be made in air-conditioned comfort in less than one day of travel using one of the miracles of modern transportation passing nearby.

We can never fully appreciate the anguish and grief experienced by this family as they traveled through strange country over rough dirt trails while doing their best to provide comfort and care to a young child suffering a life-threatening illness. It is not difficult to imagine their feelings of desperation, isolation and helplessness as they watched the life of their child slowly slip away.

Amid their sorrow, Sheriff Thomas Williams performed a remarkable act of compassion and kindness to a family of strangers. He offered a beautiful and peaceful place for a young girl to be laid to rest among members of his own family. For the remainder of their days, this one extraordinary act of kindness would provide a sense of closure and comfort for her parents in knowing their daughter would never again be alone, even in death.

In many ways, this story begins and ends in a cemetery nestled among the majestic oak trees atop the crest of a small hill near the once-thriving community of Jumbo. But for the compassion of Thomas H. Williams, the first sheriff of Chilton County, the story of an unknown girl whose journey in life came to a tragic end on the trail to South Carolina would have been forever consigned to the unwritten pages of history.

The Cedar Grove

Located on top of a small ridge along County Road 45 near Stanton, Ebenezer Cemetery serves as the final resting place for generations of families who lived on land that, over time, has been a part of four counties: Autauga, Bibb, Baker and Chilton.

In the southeast corner of this hallowed ground, a small cluster of cedar trees stands in stark contrast to the majestic oaks and longleaf pines that surround the cemetery. This small group of cedar trees seems out of place among the rows of marble monuments that serve to remind us of those whose lives have passed into history.

In the Bible, the prophet Ezekiel has a vision in which God speaks: "In the mountain of the height of Israel will I plant it: and it shall bring forth boughs, and bear fruit, and be a goodly cedar; and under it shall dwell all fowl of every wing; in the shadow of the branches thereof shall they dwell."

The cedar is mentioned more often and held in higher regard than any other tree in the Holy Scriptures, its longevity and the perennial green of its canopy symbolic of eternal life. Because of its pleasant aroma and resistance to decay, wood of the cedar was often used to assemble caskets and funeral pyres for the great rulers of antiquity. Cedar was also used in the construction of gates that safeguarded temples and burial grounds to protect and preserve the passage between life and death. In *Stories in Stone: A Field Guide to Cemetery Symbolism*, author Douglas Keister relates that the cedar tree has been associated with death and immortality throughout history.

At the foot of the aging trees, a memorial erected in November 1977 by the Chilton County chapter of the United Daughters of the Confederacy serves as a testament to a remarkable story of compassion demonstrated by a Southern family caught in the ravages of the American Civil War.

In March 1865, Union forces under the command of General John H. Wilson initiated a campaign to destroy industrial and manufacturing facilities in Alabama. A primary goal of the campaign was the destruction of the Confederate ammunition arsenal at Selma. Led by General Nathan Bedford Forrest, mounted cavalry troops of the Confederate army stood as the last line of defense against the onslaught of Wilson's forces. As the Union army marched south to Ebenezer Church, the simple log home of resident Oliver Perry McGee was commandeered as a field hospital to treat Union soldiers wounded in battle. According to local historian Wayne Arnold, the interior doors of the home were removed to be used as stretchers for the injured.

This monument was erected in memory of twelve soldiers of the Union army who were killed on April 1, 1865, during the Battle of Ebenezer Church.

As described in *The Life of Nathan Bedford Forrest* by John Wyeth, the two armies engaged in a fierce battle on April 1, 1865, along an east-to-west line centered on the intersection of two small roads near Ebenezer Church. Vastly outnumbered, Forrest's men, assisted by members of the home guard, fought valiantly but were no match for the numerical superiority of the Union army. Historians believe that the battle to defend the arsenal at Selma was fought, and lost, at Ebenezer Church.

After the battle, the armies continued south in the direction of Selma, allowing McGee and his family to return to their home. As McGee assessed the damage to his property, he discovered the bodies of seven Union soldiers mortally wounded in the battle. From stories passed down through generations, Wayne Arnold relates that Annie McGee, wife of Oliver Perry McGee, directed her husband to give the men a proper burial even though it meant soldiers of the Union army would be laid to rest in Southern ground.

These seven men, with five of their fellow Union soldiers who lost their lives during the battle, were buried beside a road through what is now Ebenezer Cemetery. To memorialize the burial site, McGee planted cedar trees next to the graves. These goodly cedar trees serve as a memorial to those Union soldiers who died so far from home.

In a terrible conflict that divided families and brought brothers to arms in opposing armies, small acts of humanity created hope that the nation could heal its wounds and its citizens could again live united in a time of peace and forgiveness.

Gracing the final resting places of those who came before us, the goodly cedar stands erect, a sentinel watching over them, pointing to the heavens in remembrance of the victory over death that is a gift for all, an enduring symbol of hope and faith for mankind. Today, the small grove of cedar trees standing in the southeast corner of Ebenezer Cemetery continues to provide a sense of hope for peace and forgiveness for all mankind.

THE BLUE AND GREY COTTAGE

"I believe it is within the power of the surviving soldiers of the Great War to make fraternity a national anthem, loyalty a national creed and charity a national virtue." These words were penned in September 1902 by Eliakim Torrance, commander in chief of the Grand Army of the Republic, an organization of veterans who served in the Union army during the American Civil War. In writing of the virtues of fraternity, loyalty and charity, Torrance initiated one of the most touching and remarkable events in the history of Chilton County.

Following the end of the American Civil War, twenty-eight northern states established homes for veterans of the Union army. These facilities were funded through federal and state appropriations. Homes for veterans of the Confederate army were established in fifteen southern states and California but were funded solely through state grants and public donations.

Jefferson Manly Falkner, a Montgomery attorney and former officer in the Eighth Confederate Calvary, became the driving force behind establishing a facility to care for indigent and disabled veterans in Alabama. In February 1902, Falkner donated eighty acres of his own land located near the Mountain Creek community in southeast Chilton County for the establishment of a home for indigent veterans of the Confederate army. The site selected was considered a healthy environment for the disabled and elderly veterans because of the abundance of fresh air due to its high elevation and the numerous natural springs and creeks nearby.

Falkner organized a statewide public fund drive to finance construction of the facility. Events included dances, quilt raffles and speeches by public officials. Lumber for construction of many of the buildings was donated by local sawmills. The Louisville and Nashville Railroad transported building materials to Mountain Creek at no charge.

Although donations for construction of the facility were received from several sources, the most remarkable was that made by members of the Grand Army of the Republic. Less than four decades after the end of a war that waged brother against brother in armed conflict on the field of

The Blue and Grey Cottage at the Alabama Home for Confederate Veterans was funded by donations from the Grand Army of the Republic.

battle, this group of aging veterans of the Union army donated funds for the construction of a cottage to shelter indigent and disabled veterans of the Confederate army.

Appropriately, the cottage was named the Blue and Grey Cottage in honor of the fraternity of veterans whose loyalty to a nation still healing from conflict was demonstrated by an enduring sense of charity to a group of former adversaries.

The Alabama Home for Confederate Veterans would grow to encompass twenty-two structures that included ten cottages, an administration building, a twenty-five-bed hospital and a mess hall. The staff included the commandant, a physician, a nurse, laborers and domestic workers. During its thirty-seven years of operation, as many as eight hundred veterans and their wives or widows resided at the home. In June 1934, the sole remaining veteran in residence at the home passed away. In October 1939, the five remaining widows were transferred to the state welfare department, and the facility at Mountain Creek was closed.

Among the former veterans and their wives who resided at the Old Soldier's Home, as it was more familiarly known, more than three hundred chose to remain and now rest in peace in that hallowed ground. Their memory is a reminder not only of a war that divided a nation but also of the healing hands of brotherhood and friendship extended between former adversaries, a timeless lesson of fraternity, loyalty and charity among citizens of the United States of America.

The Tragic Death of Andrew Jackson Langston

Nestled among the majestic oak trees that border County Road 153 east of Jemison, the tranquility of Mount New Hope Cemetery is disturbed only by the sound of an occasional automobile. The hallowed ground that is the final resting place of the earliest settlers of the land that became Chilton County is overgrown with grass and weeds. The cemetery and the memories of the lives of the families buried in its consecrated ground have become obscured by the passage of time.

Seemingly separated from the other markers and unmarked graves of long-forgotten ancestors is the simple granite headstone of Private Andrew Jackson Langston. Memorialized on the face of the granite are the dates of his birth, death and service in the Army of the Confederate States of America. The brief biography chiseled into the headstone fails to reveal the tragic story of his death and a disturbing period in our history.

The final resting place of Andrew Jackson Langston is in the Mount New Hope Cemetery near Jemison.

Andrew Jackson Langston was born on February 10, 1843, in Bibb County, Alabama. In April 1855, the Langston family moved to a farm located at Dry Valley in south Shelby County near what is today the Providence Baptist Church. In 1868, this land would become part of Baker and, subsequently, Chilton County.

During 1864, the last full year of the American Civil War, Langston either joined or was conscripted into the Army of the Confederate States of America and was sent to the camp of instruction at Talladega, Alabama, for basic military training. Not much is known about his service in the Confederate army, but in

December 1864, Langston returned home on furlough after reportedly being wounded in battle.

After four long years of civil war, residents of Alabama and other Southern states had begun to accept the reality that the overwhelming strength of the Union army would eventually prevail, and the war would be lost. With each defeat on the battlefield, enlistments and conscription of personnel continued to decrease, while the rate of desertions of frontline soldiers increased dramatically.

By the spring of 1864, assemblies of local men known as the home guard were authorized to enforce conscription laws and return deserters to military service. Captains of the home guard were afforded almost unlimited authority without provisions for providing basic constitutional protections for the accused. An individual considered to be a deserter or otherwise attempting to avoid military service would be captured, convicted and often sentenced to death by hanging without benefit of a trial. In some districts, Confederate soldiers on leave with valid furlough documents were not safe from the vigilante actions of the home guard.

The region known as Lower Yellowleaf for the creek that traversed the land became an ideal refuge for military deserters and those attempting to avoid arrest by home guard conscripting officers. Located in the northern half of present-day Chilton County, the area was sparsely populated by yeoman farmers and their families. Broken only by shallow creeks and small isolated farms, the wooded hills and valleys of the Lower Yellowleaf provided a haven for those seeking sanctuary from military service.

Typically, the home guard consisted of men exempted from the conscription laws or former soldiers disabled by wounds or disease. In some cases, however, self-appointed groups consisting of the most ruthless criminal elements assumed this role. In the fall of 1864, members of the Blackwell Crowd, a group described as the roughest and most heartless men that could be found, rode into the Lower Yellowleaf region and initiated a reign of terror over individuals and families considered to be Union loyalists or those who provided a safe haven for deserters.

The leader of the group, Robert B. Blackwell, came to Alabama from Shelbyville, Tennessee. Blackwell identified himself as having the rank of major and claimed to have orders to arrest deserters and Union sympathizers, even though he had no connection to the Confederate government. In Tennessee, Blackwell had initiated his own guerilla war against Federal troops and had been accused of murdering a Confederate army officer who attempted to enlist Blackwell and his accomplices.

The Blackwell Crowd arrived in the Lower Yellowleaf area during October 1864 after fleeing across the Tennessee River into Alabama. Soon after their arrival, they began attacking farms of families suspected of harboring army deserters and those sympathetic to the Union. The Blackwell Crowd burned houses and barns, stole livestock and terrorized the residents of Lower Yellowleaf. The Blackwell Crowd would ultimately be blamed for the murders of seventeen suspected Confederate army deserters and Union sympathizers.

On December 15, 1864, Andrew Jackson Langston married Martha Elmira Cobb in Shelby, Alabama. On February 6, 1865, less than two months after the wedding and four days before his twenty-second birthday, Langston and his father, Willis, whose opposition to the war was well known among his neighbors, were abducted from their home by members of the Blackwell Crowd. Father and son were hanged from the same tree only a short distance from their farm. Four days later, these self-proclaimed vigilantes returned to Dry Valley and murdered the father of Andrew Langston's bride, Charles B. Cobb.

After burying her husband, father and father-in-law, the young widow Martha Langston allegedly stated that trouble would never defeat her. Having experienced the murders of three members of her family, she could survive anything. In 1866, Martha Langston married Confederate war veteran Felix James Seales. On December 26, 1921, the mother of six children preceded her husband in death and was buried in the Maplesville Cemetery. On her headstone is a tribute: "Rest Mother, Rest in Quiet Sleep, While Children in Sorrow O'er Thee Weep."

During the chaotic years following the end of the American Civil War, legal authority throughout the South was virtually nonexistent until military law was imposed during the early years of Reconstruction. No member of the Blackwell Crowd was ever charged with a crime or required to answer for their actions in a court of law.

Ironically, stories passed down through generations relate that some members of the Blackwell Crowd were killed by local vigilante groups in retaliation for the deaths of their loved ones. The leader of the notorious group, Robert Blackwell, left Alabama for Texas after the war but was murdered soon after arriving in the Lone Star State.

The tragic death of Andrew Jackson Langston serves as a constant reminder of the atrocities associated with armed conflict. In wars large and small, casualties often include the innocent. In reflecting on the death of Andrew Jackson Langston and others like him who perished on a battlefield not occupied by opposing armies, perhaps the words of historian Howard Zinn are most appropriate: "There is no flag large enough to cover the shame of killing innocent people."

The Prayer of the Bell

On the eleventh hour of the eleventh day of the eleventh month of 1918, the devastation of the First World War mercifully came to an end. Author and social commentator H.G. Wells referred to this first global conflict as "the war to end all wars," a reference that would prove to be not only overly optimistic but also tragically inaccurate.

The destruction and carnage of the First World War was unprecedented in world history. Military and civilian casualties have been estimated at more than forty million killed and wounded. Families across the United States endured the loss of loved ones, including the families of thirty young men of Chilton County who gave their last full measure of devotion on the fields of France.

The war was never far from the minds of the residents of the small community of Verbena. According to an article published in the *Birmingham News* in 1918, the bell of the Methodist church would ring each afternoon at six o'clock for approximately two minutes. As the sound of the bell resonated through the community, the people of Verbena would cease whatever they were doing for a moment of prayer.

"With heads uncovered and bowed, each man, woman, child, saint and sinner repeats these words: God bless our President, our soldiers and the Nation, and guide them to victory." When the tolling of the bell was heard, "men would stop in the street; wagons would be pulled up on the road; women would rise from their knitting or pause in their cookery—for they have early supper in Verbena—the plowman halts his work, and each person repeats the prayer."

The people of Verbena called this observance the Prayer of the Bell, and it was said that men who had never before been known to pray would dutifully answer its call.

With the end of the war in November 1918, the world was once again at peace, and the bell went silent. In December 1941, as the armed forces of the United States were mobilized for a Second World War, Verbena resident Sidney Lanier Gibson immediately called for the ringing of the bell to resume.

During the First and Second World War, the bell of the Verbena Methodist Church would call residents to prayer each day.

When an article appeared in the *London Times* describing the ringing of the bell in Verbena, Gibson received a letter from a member of the British Royal Air Force who expressed the gratitude of the airmen of his squadron for the prayers of comfort and peace offered by the people of Verbena. The letter, signed only "Wellington," concluded, "God bless and have faith in us for we are in good heart."

Not far from the Verbena Methodist Church and the bell that called the community to prayer during two world wars, a modest monument was erected to memorialize the Alabama boys of Chilton County killed in the war of 1914–18. The names of thirty young men are inscribed on the face of the plaque as a reminder of those who answered the call of their nation and fought and died in a foreign land more than one hundred years ago.

The tolling of a bell is the traditional method of offering respect and honor to those who have fallen in the service of their fellow citizens. In Chilton County, each toll of the bell is symbolic of the honor and respect earned by those whose names are inscribed on the face of the veterans' memorial in Clanton and whose memory shall forever remain in the hearts of those they served.

A War within a War

In October 1918, the *Union Banner* published a cryptic poem that read, in part, "When your tonsils squeak and your hair gets dry; and you are doggone certain that you are going to die; but you're scared you won't and afraid you will; just drag to bed and have your chill; and pray the Lord will see you through; for you have the flu boy, you have the flu."

The poem was published during the Spanish Influenza pandemic that infected more than five hundred million people worldwide. First appearing in the spring of 1918, the virus became dormant after only a few months. As summer transitioned to fall, the virus mutated and returned with a vengeance. Before abating, the pandemic would claim more than fifty million lives.

Residents of Chilton County were not safe from the dreaded contagion. During the final week of October 1918, the *Union Banner* reported, "The influenza is raging in this city and section with seven deaths and funerals reported since Saturday night." The article noted the sudden death of Clanton postmaster J.E. Robinson from the "cruel influenza that bested all that medical skill and kind friends could do."

The rapid spread of the disease has been attributed to the massive mobilization and deployment of soldiers for service in Europe during the First World War. Military training camps and troop transport ships served as breeding grounds for the virus, which quickly spread among closely quartered soldiers and sailors. In the United States, more than thirty thousand American soldiers would be lost to influenza in training camps.

Left: The headstone of Perry Sanford Edwards, who died of influenza on October 17, 1918, at Camp Hancock, Georgia.

Right: Ernest Clinton Edwards died of influenza in France one week before his brother. The brothers rest beside each other in the Isabella Cemetery.

In July 1918, Perry Sanford Edwards of the Isabella community was inducted into the U.S. Army at Camp Hancock, Georgia. Nine days after his induction into the military, Edwards learned that he had become the father of a baby girl. His letters home were filled with his desire to see his new daughter. Because Edwards was unable to return to Isabella, his wife, Ava Jewel, decided to travel to Georgia to allow her husband to see their child.

Arriving at Camp Hancock in October 1918, the young mother was turned away. A quarantine order had been put into effect because of an outbreak of influenza. Returning to Isabella, Ava Jewel made plans to return as soon as the quarantine was lifted.

Only days after returning home, Ava Jewell received a telegram advising that her husband was seriously ill with pneumonia. The following day, a second telegram informed her of his death. Only twenty-three years of age, Perry Edwards was laid to rest in the Isabella Cemetery; his grave adorned with a marble tombstone that reads, "A kind wife mourns in thee, a husband lost."

The obituary for Perry Edwards was published in the *Union Banner* the following week. The notice listed the surviving members of the family, including his older brother Ernest Clinton Edwards, "now in France serving with the American Expeditionary Forces." Tragically, the obituary was written before the family received notification that Ernest Edwards had died ten days earlier from the same disease that claimed the life of his younger brother.

Perry and Ernest Edwards were soldiers who lost their lives in service to their country. Even though the brothers did not fall in armed conflict, their lives were lost to an equally lethal adversary. Their legacy is a constant reminder of the threats of war and disease, enemies of humanity that must be vanquished.

Eleanora

In 1977, author Alex Haley was awarded a Special Citation Pulitzer Prize for his book *Roots*, a work of historical fiction that chronicled the lives of his maternal ancestors from Gambia in West Africa to the antebellum plantations of the American South. The book became a cultural sensation and was adapted for television, becoming the most popular miniseries in history.

During the decade that followed the publication of *Roots*, Haley began conducting research for a similar project. Based on the life of his paternal grandmother, the book and subsequent miniseries *Queen: The Story of An American Family* were released in 1993, one year after Haley's death.

Born in 1857 in Lauderdale County, Alabama, Queen was the daughter of Easter, a young enslaved woman who lived and worked on a plantation near Florence. The owner of the plantation, James Jackson Jr., had become involved in a relationship with Easter, a relationship that led to the birth of Queen, Alex Haley's grandmother.

A central theme of the book is the relationship between Queen and her half sister Eleanora. Although fictitious names are used in the book, the real Eleanora Hickman Jackson, known to family and friends as Nora, was born in December 1858 in Florence. Before her death, the life of Eleanora Hickman Jackson would become closely intertwined with Chilton County.

Eleanora was born into a world of turmoil and tragedy. In addition to the emotional issues that existed in the lives of her parents, Eleanora was only two years of age when the Alabama legislature approved the Ordinance of Secession from the Union of States. In April 1861, her father left home to enlist in the Fourth Alabama Infantry Regiment. Young Eleanora did not see him again for four years.

Of the seven Jackson children, only Eleanora, her brother Robert and her half sister Queen lived beyond the age of seven. After the premature death of her mother in 1872, Eleanora was enrolled at the Synodical College in Florence, an institution of religious education. In January 1887, Eleanora married William Henry Phillips of Loachapoka in Lee County. The young couple moved to Clanton to join William's brother, local merchant Thomas Smart Phillips. William and Eleanora lived a quiet life in Clanton. According to genealogical research conducted by family descendants, William was employed as a druggist. He and Eleanora attended the local Baptist church.

However, the turmoil and tragedy that seemed a continuing presence in Eleanora's life reemerged in August 1894. After only seven years of marriage, her husband William died at forty-three years of age. He was buried at the Clanton Cemetery in a modest grave adorned with a simple marker.

Following the death of her husband, Eleanora left Clanton to live in Bessemer, Alabama. She never remarried and never returned to reside at the Forks of the Cypress, the family home in Florence. For the remainder of her years, Eleanora quietly sought the peace and serenity that seemed lacking

The final resting place of Eleanora Jackson Phillips in the Clanton Cemetery. Her family was the subject of the book *Queen* by author Alex Haley.

for much of her life. On August 20, 1937, the forty-third anniversary of the death of her husband, Eleanora found the peace that had evaded her for so long. Eleanora was laid to rest with William, her name engraved below that of her husband on the stone ledger placed in his memory.

The legacy of Eleanora Jackson Phillips is best expressed by the words of Linda Goetsch: "Remember me in the family tree; my name, my days, my strife. Then I'll ride upon the wings of time and live an endless life."

Double Play

In a 1946 interview published in the *Chicago Tribune*, former Chicago White Sox pitcher Sam Jones stated, "If I was pitching a game for the championship of the world and the outcome depended on one play, I would want it to be a ground ball to Jackie Hayes."

Minter Carney "Jackie" Hayes was born on July 19, 1906, in Clanton. During high school, Hayes demonstrated his natural athletic ability by earning varsity letters in football, basketball and baseball. After graduation, Hayes played collegiate baseball for the University of Alabama and earned a reputation as a dependable fielder with a special talent for turning double plays. Teammates always referred to Hayes as Jackie, never Minter.

After two years at the University of Alabama, Hayes was offered a fabulous salary of $25,000 a year to play professional baseball for the Washington Senators. In 1932, Hayes was traded to the Chicago White Sox, where he spent the remainder of his nine years as a professional athlete. As a member of the White Sox, Hayes would play against the greatest legends of baseball, including Lou Gehrig, Dizzy Dean and the "Yankee Clipper," Joe DiMaggio.

During the 1937 season, Jackie Hayes led Major League Baseball in double plays. Former Washington teammate and Baseball Hall of Fame inductee Joe Cronin called Hayes the finest double-play second baseman in professional baseball. Hayes further distinguished himself in 1940 by being the first player in the history of professional baseball to wear a batting helmet during a game. Hayes had designed and constructed the headgear himself.

In 1940, Jackie Hayes began suffering the debilitating effects of glaucoma, first losing vision in his right eye. Although he managed to play in eighteen games that year, the disease would eventually end his major league career. Three years later, glaucoma destroyed the vision in his left eye, leaving the finest double-play second baseman in baseball completely blind.

Loss of vision is a catastrophic life event that can lead to depression and create other significant obstacles to living a full and rewarding life. According to Hall of Fame pitcher Ted Lyons, "Jackie Hayes was a man who would not give up. He didn't care what the score was. If our team trailed by ten runs, he would hustle just as much in the ninth inning as he did in the first." This "never quit" view of life would be a major influence in the future success of Jackie Hayes.

Top: Minter Carney (Jackie) Hayes was described as the finest double-play second baseman in professional baseball.

Bottom: Hayes and his service dog Abano attended Jackie Hayes Day at Comiskey Park in Chicago during a White Sox home game.

Following his retirement from professional baseball, Hayes returned to Clanton and was soon elected to the office of tax collector. With the able assistance of his wife Alice Brooks Hayes, the former White Sox second baseman would serve three terms in office. For the remainder of his life, Hayes also continued to enjoy sports, participating in golf tournaments sponsored by the Blind Golfers Association.

In August 1946, the Chicago White Sox hosted Jackie Hayes Day at Comiskey Park. Former teammate Ted Lyons recalled that "Hayes sat around the clubhouse with the players before the game. He always knew who was talking because he could recognize their voices after he heard them speak a couple of times."

Jack Hayes was once asked how blindness affected his life. He thoughtfully responded, "Don't feel sorry for me. Being blind has its compensations. I never knew before how kind and thoughtful even strangers can be. Those with sight see everything and some of the things they see aren't very pretty. I am able to visualize things and I can make them as beautiful as I like." Not unlike a hard-hit ground ball, the life of Jackie Hayes took a bad bounce. However, as he had done so many times, he turned a challenge into a double play. In February 1976, in recognition of his many accomplishments, Minter Carney Hayes was inducted into the Alabama Sports Hall of Fame. Bart Starr, quarterback of the world champion Green Bay Packers football team, was also an inductee. The baseball park in downtown Clanton is also named in his honor.

Minter Carney "Jackie" Hayes passed away on February 9, 1983, and was laid to rest in the Clanton Cemetery. It is fitting that his first and most faithful service dog, Abano, rests peacefully at the foot of his grave.

The Day the Music Died

"There is nothing in God's world more beautiful than Alabama's woods and hills, in early summer. The landscape, dressed in lush green, and the light blue haze that shadows the peaks, give you a feeling of awe at the magnificence of God's creation." James Blackwood, founding member and lead vocalist of the Blackwood Brothers Quartet, penned these words as he recalled the June 30, 1954 flight onboard the group's Beechcraft Model 18 aircraft bound for Clanton, Alabama. The quartet, one of the most renowned southern gospel groups in the nation, was scheduled to perform as the main attraction at the annual Chilton County Peach Festival being held at the Chilton County Airport.

Established in 1947, the Chilton County Peach Festival was created to recognize the region's agricultural industry, especially local peach growers. J. Archie Ogburn, civic leader and member of the board of directors of the Bank of Thorsby, was instrumental in organizing the festival and served as its first general chairman. Except for 1951, the countywide celebration had been held on an annual basis and had become the region's most eagerly anticipated community event. The 1954 celebration was advertised as the biggest and best peach festival, and the marquee events included an agricultural exposition, hillbilly singing and wrestling matches featuring Rowdy Red Roberts, former southern junior heavyweight champion.

The airport's large metal hangar had been converted into an auditorium and concert hall with a stage erected at one end. Seats were brought in to accommodate crowds attending events that included the crowning of the 1954 peach festival queen. Thirty-five young women competing for the title would be judged by representatives of five Alabama colleges. Popular Albertville radio commentator Jessie Culp served as master of ceremonies. Dressing rooms were constructed adjacent to the hangar for the contestants and other peach festival performers. The area outside of the hangar was converted into a cow palace, a showplace for cattle and other livestock. Workers also completed construction of a display area for local agricultural products.

The headline of the *Union Banner* was almost prophetic in describing the concert that would culminate six big days and nights of the festival: "Entertainment the like of which Chilton County has never seen before is in store until Wednesday night." On that last night of the peach festival celebration, two of the most outstanding gospel quartets in the nation, the Blackwood Brothers and the Statesmen, were scheduled to perform in the recently converted hangar at the Chilton County Airport.

Formed in 1934 in Choctaw County, Mississippi, during the Great Depression, the Blackwood Brothers Quartet originally performed in local churches, where they would charge a nickel for concerts. Original members of the group included brothers James, Doyle and Roy Blackwood. The fourth member of the quartet was Roy's son, thirteen-year-old baritone R.W. Blackwood. After moving to Memphis, Tennessee, in 1950, the Blackwood Brothers' fame spread as they began to appear on radio and television stations throughout the southeast. Fellow musician and Mississippi native Elvis Presley was a huge fan of gospel music and especially admired the Blackwood Brothers.

By 1954, several members of the original quartet had retired or left the group. Just two weeks before their Clanton performance, the Blackwood Brothers lineup of Bill Shaw (tenor), James Blackwood (lead), R.W. Blackwood (baritone), Bill Lyles (bass) and Jackie Marshall (piano) won the Arthur Godfrey Talent Scouts competition on national television with their stirring rendition of the gospel classic "Have You Talked to the Man Upstairs?"

As their popularity grew and their concert schedule became more demanding, the group decided to begin utilizing an airplane for their travel needs, reasoning that travel by air would be much more convenient and less fatiguing than riding in the large automobiles that gospel groups typically used as their means of transportation. From 1952 until 1954, the group owned several different airplanes before purchasing a ten-passenger, twin-engine Beechcraft Model 18. R.W. Blackwood piloted the aircraft while Bill Lyles served as copilot and navigator.

James Blackwood would later remember the flight from their last performance in Gulfport, Mississippi, to Clanton as a beautiful experience, "Cruising at six thousand feet, the motors of our plane were humming a soothing, muted lullaby. Wisps of fleecy, white clouds were here and there,

Right: The Blackwood Brothers gospel quartet was scheduled to perform at the Chilton County Airport as the concluding event of the 1954 peach festival.

Below: Pilot R.W. Blackwood (*left*) and copilot Bill Lyles took off in the group's twin-engine Beechcraft airplane for a test flight minutes before their scheduled appearance.

around us." Arriving in Clanton at noon, James recalled being greeted by hundreds of their Chilton County fans, many of whom had been awaiting their arrival since early morning. After an hour of shaking hands, signing autographs and greeting admirers, the group was ushered into the large hangar where the concert was to be held. Although the formal program was not scheduled to begin until seven o'clock, the group did give a short, informal performance during a luncheon hosted by the Lions Club, sponsors of the evening concert.

In 1954, the Chilton County Airport consisted of two sod runways, one oriented in an east–west direction with the second running northwest to southeast. Neither runway was equipped with lights for night takeoffs or landings. Since the group planned to return to Memphis immediately following the concert, a night takeoff on the unlighted runway would be required. Typically, automobiles would be parked along the sides of the runway and their headlights used to illuminate the takeoff area. At approximately six fifteen, forty-five minutes before their concert was scheduled to begin, R.W. Blackwood decided that he and copilot Bill Lyles would make a test flight to get the lay of the field so that he would have no trouble taking off later that evening.

As they boarded the airplane, Blackwood and Lyles were joined on the flight by Johnny Ogburn Jr., the twenty-year-old son and namesake of the founder of the Chilton County Peach Festival. Following graduation from high school, Ogburn had joined the United States Air Force and served as an airman second class at Kesseler Field, Biloxi, Mississippi. He was married to the former Peggy Joyce Noah, and the couple had celebrated their first anniversary the previous week.

A crowd assembled to watch the takeoff. Inside the airplane, R.W. Blackwood and Bill Lyles could be seen in the pilot compartment, while young Johnny Ogburn waved as he peered through a window in the passenger cabin. Shortly, the engines roared to life, and the airplane begin to taxi to the end of the runway for takeoff. Because the wind had shifted since the time of their arrival, the takeoff and subsequent landing would be in the opposite direction from that used during their earlier arrival. This required the airplane to overfly a small hill during the landing approach. After clearing the hill, it would be necessary for the pilot to reduce speed and lose altitude quickly enough to touch down and stop on the short grass runway.

Dusk had fallen as the twin-engine Beechcraft began its takeoff. James Blackwood would later write that "twilight is for being with friends and family, for rest, for songs and for courting, but not the time for landing a large airplane on short and tricky landing strips." The spectators watched intently as R.W. Blackwood circled the field several times, then maneuvered the big airplane into the landing pattern. After clearing the small hill at the end of the runway, the pilot lowered the nose of the airplane forcefully, but the machine gathered speed and was moving too fast to land.

Realizing that insufficient runway remained, Blackwood pushed the throttles forward, retracted the landing gear and began a climb to enter the landing pattern for a second attempt. The assembled crowd, not understanding the drama that was unfolding before them, remained in a holiday mood, cheering and waving as the airplane climbed overhead.

Approaching the runway on the second attempt to land, James Blackwood observed the airplane clear the hill as the pilot began a sideslip maneuver to reduce speed and lose altitude rapidly. Touching down, the Beechcraft bounced back into the air. As before, R.W. Blackwood applied power to initiate a go-around maneuver to climb back into the air for another attempt to land.

Almost immediately, the crowd began to sense that something was terribly wrong as nose of the big airplane continued to rise into an almost vertical climb. Watching in horror, James Blackwood thought it was as though a giant, invisible hand was pulling a toy airplane up on a string. Then, as if in slow motion, the airplane seemed to hang suspended for a moment, neither climbing nor falling, before it appeared to gracefully turn and dive viciously into the ground.

As a young man, future Clanton mayor Billy Joe Driver was sitting on the last row of bleachers inside the hangar waiting for the Blackwood Brothers Quartet performance to begin. He recalled,

> *From my seat, I could see the airplane as it approached for landing. Although I couldn't say why, it just didn't look right to me. I could see the airplane as it began to climb. It appeared to go straight up into the air. It looked like it was going to do a loop maneuver, but it nosed down and descended into the ground. At first, I thought it was some kind of prank, but suddenly people were running out of the hangar onto the landing field. We just couldn't believe what had happened. It didn't seem real.*

According to the *Union Banner*, within seconds of the accident, "all was bedlam on the airport." Because of the traffic congestion associated with the peach festival, the fire department and ambulances had a difficult time responding to the accident. The three occupants of the aircraft, R.W. Blackwood, James W. (Bill) Lyles and John Archie Ogburn Jr., were fatally injured.

A memorial to accident victims R.W. Blackwood, James W. Lyles and John A. Ogburn was erected at the Chilton County Airport.

Later in the evening, at the request of Erskin Popwell and Harold Foshee, more than one thousand people gathered at the Chilton County Airport. The assembled group voted that all the money collected from the sale of tickets to the Blackwood Brothers concert would be turned over to the families of the victims of the accident. However, anyone who was not satisfied could get their money back. No one stepped forward to request a refund. In the days that followed, a local newspaper stated that "all of Chilton County grieves with the families of the three men who died in the airplane crash."

On July 2, 1954, thousands of mourners gathered at the City Auditorium in Memphis for the funeral service for R.W. Blackwood and Bill Lyles, the largest the city had ever seen. Tennessee governor Frank Clement, who spoke "as a friend of the singers and not as Governor," recalled that he had been with the quartet when they made their last public appearance in Memphis. At his request, the mourners sang "Have You Talked to the Man Upstairs?," the song with which they won the Arthur Godfrey Talent Scouts competition. During the service, the Reverend James F. Hamill, the singers' pastor, said "a sermon to eulogize Blackwood and Lyles was as unnecessary as improving the beauty of a sunset." On that same day, the funeral service for John Archie Ogburn Jr. was held at the Thorsby Baptist Church. He was laid to rest in the Clanton Cemetery.

The accident that claimed the lives of R.W. Blackwood, Bill Lyles and Johnny Ogburn has been described as "the crash that changed the course of gospel music." Although more than six decades have passed, the memory of that day remains vivid for many residents of Clanton and Chilton County. In June 2001, the Clanton Lions Club erected a pavilion around the memorial commemorating the accident victims. From time to time, people gather at the memorial, alone or in groups, to pause for a moment to remember, to reflect and to pray.

Chapter 5
The Unique and Unusual

Hidden within every community history are stories of people and events that are unique and unusual. With the passage of time, these stories almost seem too outlandish to be true; yet these unique and unusual stories are equally important in defining the character and identity of a community.

The Possum King

Frank Basil Clark had a simple outlook on life: "I put possums first and everything else falls right into place." A native of Hanging Dog, North Carolina, Clark moved to Chilton County to manage the Clanton Drive-In Theatre. Around Clanton, Clark was known for his prominent mustache, cowboy hat, snakeskin boots and hand-tooled belt buckle engraved with his name bordered by a pair of possums.

Chilton County news editor T.E. Wyatt wrote that Clark's pleasant smile and quick wit soon led the people to accept him as homefolk. By 1976, Clark had become so well known that residents of Clanton elected him to his first of two consecutive terms as mayor.

As mayor, Clark kept a pet possum in his office at City Hall. He was quick to correct visitors who used the term *opossum*, insisting the first letter was silent. Official business was frequently delayed as he described the health benefits of a possum diet. In *Save Room for Pie*, Roy Blount Jr. relates that Clark was steadfast in his belief that possum is low in saturated fat and cleans arteries like a Roto-Rooter. To properly serve a possum entrée, the mayor recommended a side of sweet potatoes to complement the flavor of the meat. For the discerning palate, Clark recommended peach-fed possum, maintaining that nothing could be sweeter. Well known among the citizens of Clanton, the Possum King also achieved notoriety as founder of the International Possum Growers and Breeders Association.

Two-term Clanton mayor Frank Basil Clark was founder of the International Possum Growers and Breeders Association.

According to the *New Encyclopedia of Southern Culture*, the International Possum Growers and Breeders Association held its first national meeting in 1971 at Clanton. The association's membership list soon grew to more than forty thousand and included former presidents Carter, Reagan and George H.W. Bush. Benefits of membership included the highly popular "Eat More Possum"–themed license plate. As founder, Basil Clark practiced what he preached, offering possum burgers at the Chilton County Fair and refreshment counter of the Clanton drive-in.

The highlight of the annual membership meeting was the possum judging. Possum contestants from across the United States were judged on criteria that included configuration of the head, tail and feet. The most important category, however, was the possum's personality. At the conclusion of the judging, the winner was proclaimed the Beauregard and reigned until the next International Possum Show. The association also sponsored a pageant in conjunction with the Chilton County Fair for young women to compete for the title of Possum Queen.

The Possum Growers and Breeders Association of America and its founder, Basil Clark, became a media sensation, with articles appearing in magazines and newspapers across the country, including *Sports Illustrated*, *National Geographic* and the *New York Times*. The popularity of the possum movement peaked as Clark and Stonewall Jackson III, the international champion registered pedigreed stud possum, appeared on the popular television show *What's My Line?*.

Basil Clark epitomized the adage "You can take the boy out of the country, but you can't take the country out of the boy." While attending a mayor's conference in Washington, D.C., Clark was able to talk his way into the Russian embassy to try to convince the Soviet government that possum breeding would solve that nation's food shortage. In exchange for two live pandas to be obtained from the People's Republic of China, which were to be displayed at the Clanton Drive-In Theatre, Clark proposed a deal to provide registered possums to start the first possum ranch in Russia.

Unfortunately, his visit occurred during the height of the Cold War. Leaving the embassy, Clark was immediately detained by federal agents for questioning. After several hours of interrogation, he was finally released. Needless to say, the first international possum exchange became a victim of Cold War politics.

Frank Basil Clark passed away in 2004. The legacy of this Chilton County original is best expressed in his own words, "A registered possum is a better possum. If people believe that, they will believe anything. A person who will believe anything can do anything." Without a doubt, Basil Clark believed not only in himself but also in his ability to do anything.

THE POSSUM GOURMET

In November 1974, a unique promotion that originated in Chilton County reached mainstream America. To coin a modern phrase, the slogan "Eat More Possum" went viral, introduced to the nation by the *New York Times* and the *Atlanta Journal*. Nationally syndicated magazines *Sports Illustrated* and *National Geographic* also provided extensive coverage of the story.

One of the driving forces behind this revolutionary concept was twenty-three-year-old Danny Eiland of Clanton, who had been raising and eating possums since he was in knee pants. According to Eiland, "Poor folks have always eaten possum but so have a lot of smart folks!"

A charter member of the International Possum Growers and Breeders Association, Eiland concentrated his efforts on culinary research, working to overcome the socioeconomic prejudice associated with the breeding of possums as a potential solution to the problem of world hunger. In time, his efforts came to fruition when he published a book of possum recipes created to appeal to even the most discerning palate. Eiland was a bona fide connoisseur of possum cuisine, and his creations included Roast Possum a la Clanton and Possum Alabama.

One of the biggest challenges in promoting possum meat as a delicacy is the natural tendency of some folks to consider the possum as nothing more than a varmint. According to one local possum authority who prefers

A charter member of the International Possum Growers and Breeders Association, Danny Eiland published a book of possum recipes. *Danny Eiland.*

to remain anonymous, "The real reason people won't eat possum is the idea of a possum. They don't want to have nothing to do with it. I just don't tell them what it is and cook it; they will beat you to the table to eat it."

Writing in *Sports Illustrated*, Roy Blount Jr. describes possum as tasting like the dark meat of chicken, only stronger tasting and looser on the bone and stringy, like pork. Others have described the taste as chicken combined with roast pork. The article does caution readers, "Wild possum could taste like anything since they eat almost everything from berries to carrion." Regardless of how it is perceived, Danny Eiland points out that possum meat is low in saturated fat and is a natural defense against the ill effects of elevated levels of cholesterol.

As a culinary master, Eiland prefers cage-fed possum for its superior taste and recommends feeding the possum liver-flavored Purina Cat Chow, supplemented with plenty of apples, peaches and persimmons, plus an occasional tidbit of cheddar cheese. According to promotional material provided by the International Possum Growers and Breeders Association, "Nothing is sweeter than a peach fed possum."

Being a possum gourmet can be hazardous. Eiland cautions using extreme care in handling the cute yet excitable marsupials. "If you reach into a box for one of them, it can be like grabbing the wrong end of a chain saw." Eiland still has a small scar on his right hand to prove his point.

In 1976, Eiland and other members of the Chilton County possum alliance exported three pounds of the succulent meat to Chicago for a formal dinner hosted by the Virginia Chemical Company. Prepared by Bo Littleton at Pig Headley's Food Center in Clanton, the special cargo was transported to the Montgomery airport and placed on an Eastern Airlines flight to Chicago. Upon arrival in the Windy City, this southern delicacy was served with a garnish complemented with a side of sweet potatoes at the Café Bohemia, an upscale restaurant located in the Loop District.

More than four decades have elapsed since a group of Chilton County visionaries introduced possum into the mainstream of American cuisine. With the Iran hostage crisis, gasoline shortages and other social upheavals of the period, however, Danny Eiland concedes that the concept was ahead of its time. The public simply wasn't ready for the paradigm shift from traditional chicken and beef dishes to possum as the protein of choice.

Today, Danny Eiland focuses his breeding and culinary expertise on the poultry industry. Although he accepts the reality that chicken tenders and nuggets have maintained their supremacy as a staple of the American diet, he eagerly anticipates the day that possum biscuits and burgers are included on the menu of every respectable restaurant in the United States—or at least in Chilton County. He even has an idea for a new slogan: "Possum: it's what's for dinner!"

The Highest Honor

In an early episode of the popular television series *The Beverly Hillbillies*, Jed, Granny, Jethro and Ellie Mae Clampett make plans to return home to Bug Tussle in the hills of Tennessee for the annual Possum Day festival. In addition to the possum parade, the Clampetts look forward to their favorite Possum Day events: the rock-slinging and mud-rasslin' contests and the crawdad-eating competition. The most anticipated event of the festival is the crowning of the Possum Queen. Uncle Jed, patriarch of the Clampett clan, opines, "Being Possum Queen is about the highest honor that can come to a woman."

For Jann Satterwhite, that "highest honor" became a reality at the 1973 Chilton County Possum Corral, which was held in conjunction with the Fourth of July celebration at Lay Dam on the Coosa River. The all-day affair included a barbecue lunch, music and, of course, presentation of the 1973 possum queens.

The daughter of former Chilton County commissioner Curtis Satterwhite, Jann graduated in 1972 from Jemison High School. As Miss Possum Queen International, Satterwhite was attended by the possum queen court of Junior Miss Possum Beverly Beadlecomb and Miss Possum of Alabama Jo Ann Jones.

Jann Satterwhite (Caton) recalls that her reign as Miss Possum Queen International was not all glitz and glamour. Instead of luxurious evening gowns, possum queens were typically adorned in outfits similar to those worn

An appearance by the reigning possum queen often involved spending the day with one of the celebrated marsupials. *Chilton County News.*

by Ellie Mae Clampett in *The Beverly Hillbillies*. Their ensemble included frayed, knee-length dresses or a plaid shirt, blue jeans and boots.

Special appearances by the possum queens at community events were seldom routine. During a late summer trip to Dothan for an appearance at the annual peanut festival, Satterwhite and her court were squeezed into the backseat of a car driven by Frank Basil Clark, president of the International Possum Growers and Breeders Association.

Before leaving Chilton County, Clark loaded two of his prize possums into the trunk of the car. Each time the car hit a bump in the road, the possums would begin to fight. The noise from the trunk sounded like two cats fighting during a tornado. As soon as the possums would settle down, the car would hit another bump, and the ruckus would begin anew, increasing in intensity with each round.

Because the car had no air-conditioning, the trip was made with the windows rolled down. When they arrived in Dothan, the newly coiffed hair of the queen and her court had lost that beauty shop look because of the near–tropical storm winds in the rear seat.

During these special appearances, the possum queens would follow Basil Clark as he strolled through the crowd with his show possums on a leash. Caton recalled that the possums fascinated most people, each having been carefully bathed and groomed prior to the appearance. However, the reigning Miss Possum Queen International could never bring herself to hold one of the celebrated marsupials.

The following year, the possum queen concept gained nationwide notoriety as Junior Miss Possum Queen Joni Hays appeared with Basil Clark on the nationally syndicated television series *To Tell the Truth*. Hays and Clark were accompanied on the trip to New York City by Stonewall Jackson III, the international champion registered pedigreed stud possum.

In retrospect, the notion of a possum queen in Chilton County was a concept ahead of its time. Today, National Possum Day is celebrated across the United States, with communities in several states now hosting possum festivals and pageants. As they say, imitation is the sincerest form of flattery.

The Trial of the Century

In the fall of 1904, an atmosphere of dissension and disunity descended upon the residents of Chilton County like a thick blanket of fog settling along the banks of the Coosa River. The source of the discord that divided friends and families alike was not politics, religion nor simmering animosities left over from the Civil War. The fervor that swept across the land came about because of one of the most famous civil trials in the history of Chilton County.

Before the trial concluded, thousands of dollars would be expended on legal fees and the court system tied up for weeks, with more than one hundred witnesses called to testify, while dozens of fistfights ensued on the steps of the courthouse and inside the courtroom.

In an effort to explain the legalities of the dispute to readers, a reporter for the *Union Banner* in Clanton wrote, "Dr. V. O. Campbell is, or was, the proud owner of a pointer dog named Frank. Mr. J. M. Robinson of Union Grove is, or was, the proud owner of a pointer dog named Hank. Robinson says that Campbell has got his dog Hank, but Campbell says it ain't so, it's his dog Frank."

Individuals described as more or less experts on the dog question were called as witnesses in the case. After several days of testimony, local newspapers described the proceedings as "such a doggone mixing up of dogs and evidence the world has seldom seen. Justice of the Peace E. B. Deason, who we all know is not much of a dog man himself, is nearly driven crazy with the doggone question and has asked for additional time to arrive at a verdict."

According to Justice Deason, "All I know is this: If the dog ain't Frank, it's Hank, and if it ain't Hank, it's Frank; if it ain't Frank or Hank, then it stands to reason that it is just another doggone dog." When he concluded his deliberations, Deason ruled in favor of Campbell. Robinson's attorney immediately filed an appeal to the circuit court.

During an era in which ownership of a prized bird dog was a source of immense pride and elevated the reputation and public standing of the owner to that of a celebrity, the trial created an unprecedented level of interest throughout the county. The case attracted the largest crowd ever to attend a trial in the courthouse at Clanton; the courtroom was packed to capacity while one thousand people milled about outside awaiting the verdict. As the trial progressed, tempers flared, fistfights erupted and serious physical confrontations between opposing groups of supporters were averted only by the quick action of the sheriff.

After hearing arguments and considering the evidence, the jury concluded that the subject of the legal dispute was not just another doggone dog. The dog was, in fact, Hank and not Frank. Robinson, the plaintiff, was awarded possession of the canine, which was assessed at an unprecedented value of ten dollars.

The trial of the century would have one final twist. Shortly after the verdict, the dog at the center of the controversy mysteriously disappeared. Retaining the services of former sheriff Lee Hayes, a man with a reputation as a natural sleuth, Robinson invested nearly $800 in the search for his prized pointer. After weeks of investigation, the misappropriated pooch was discovered at a residence in Bessemer. Robinson had Campbell arrested on a charge of larceny. However, the grand jury, hesitant to rekindle the flame of pent-up emotions relating to the outcome of the first trial, refused to issue an indictment.

Like other high-profile cases that have divided communities across the country, the thick blanket of resentment and anger created during what became known as the Bird Dog Trial began to lift only with the passage of time. Whether the canine at the center of the controversy was actually Hank, Frank or just another doggone dog, the Chilton County trial of the century was the most doggone of all.

The Hot Well, Chilton County's Fountain of Youth

In the fall of 1885, the national *Mining and Manufacturing Journal* published an article describing an investigation conducted by geologist William Gesner into the purported recuperative powers of water from the well of Clanton businessman and landowner S.A. Blasingame.

The Hot Well, as it was locally known, gained notoriety as a curative for chronic ailments. Believers claimed the water was a miracle cure for paralysis, rheumatism and scrofula, a form of tuberculosis that affects the lymph nodes. Supposedly the water was so hot that fresh eggs lowered into the well would be cooked within ten minutes.

During his investigation, Gesner determined that the well, ten feet in diameter and thirty-five feet in depth, produced water containing saline. He believed the cause of the water's hot temperature was of subterranean origin, attributable to contact with rocks under the influence of volcanic lava.

According to the *Chilton View* newspaper, people traveled to Clanton on foot and by horse, wagon and train to immerse themselves in the celebrated water of the Hot Well. Some of the visitors came on crutches, some with their feet bound up in cloth, others in rolling chairs, only to remain a few days and be able to throw their crutches and other aids aside and go away perfectly cured.

As the number of visitors increased, S.A. Blasingame constructed a boardinghouse near the well from lumber produced at his nearby sawmill. He advertised it as within a few steps of the Hot Well, and guests could secure comfortable quarters at low rates. The rooms of the Hot Well Hotel were frequently filled with affluent guests who traveled to Clanton to partake of the healing waters.

During the spring of 1887, S.A. Blasingame sold the well and boardinghouse to Dr. A.J. Massey, a traveling dentist from the Coosa County community of Rockford. Sensing a profitable investment, Massey constructed additional housing near the well to accommodate more visitors. Unfortunately, by August 1887, the residents of Clanton and surrounding communities had begun to question the curative powers of this veritable fountain of youth.

To eliminate doubt, Dr. Massey issued a formal invitation in the *Chilton View* for everyone "far and near to attend a basket dinner at the Hot Well where he would demonstrate the genuineness of the water." A special committee was formed to certify the results of the investigation.

After three days of investigation and deliberation, the committee issued their findings. The group of mineralogists and geologists determined that the water in the well was of natural temperature and was being heated by artificial means. The source of the heat was a one-inch metal pipe connected to the steam boiler of the Blasingame sawmill. The findings of the committee, published in the *Chilton View*, caused public enthusiasm for the recuperative power of the well to cool as quickly as the temperature of the water.

Without its miraculous healing power, the renowned Hot Well became just another source of water for drinking and cooking. The legacy of the Hot Well survived in subsequent years as the former site of Chilton County's fountain of youth became known as the Round O.

The popularity of hydropathy in Chilton County did not end with the demise of the Hot Well. Soon, a mineral spring located to the east of Jemison would become the next source of curative water used to alleviate chronic ailments, but that is another story.

A Dipping Dilemma

In April 1917, the armed forces of the United States began a mobilization of soldiers and equipment for deployment to Europe to assist the British and French governments in the worldwide conflict against the German army. As this international drama was unfolding, a conflict of a different magnitude was emerging in Chilton County. At the center of the skirmish was a small parasite known as the Texas Fever Tick.

According to an October 1917 article in the *Union Banner*, "If the Kaiser believes that misery loves company, he should have a brotherly feeling for the Texas Fever Tick!" An infestation of the Texas Fever Tick earlier in the year resulted in a quarantine of cattle in Chilton and other counties in Alabama. The quarantine prohibited cattle from being transported across county or state lines until the threat of the infestation was eliminated.

Proponents of a process known as "cattle dipping" believed that herding cattle through large vats filled with a solution to kill ticks was the best method to address the problem. Opponents of the process were equally convinced that dipping cattle would create problems more serious than the tick infestation.

The editor of the *Union Banner* was inundated with letters either supporting or opposing cattle dipping. One opponent complained, "I have it on good authority from farmers in Coosa and Elmore Counties that dipping ruins the cows from milk and butter." A proponent countered, "After dipping, cattle did twenty percent better than any year before."

Even though an editorial in the *Union Banner* implored readers "not to allow this matter to become a political issue," candidates for the office of the commissioners court found themselves squarely in the middle of the debate. One letter to the editor stated, "I don't intend to help elect a candidate that is in favor of the rotten question of cattle dipping."

By December 1917, the issue had reached the point that probate judge L.H. Reynolds called for a special election to be held the following April on the question of cattle dipping. Newspaper editorials warned readers, "There is much danger in acting on the proposition without researching the facts and receiving the proper conviction."

Even though voters in Chilton County overwhelmingly defeated the referendum to impose mandatory cattle dipping, the Alabama legislature resolved the issue by adopting a statewide Tick Eradication Law that mandated the treatment of cattle. In Chilton County, eight inspectors were

During 1918, twenty-seven cattle-dipping vats were being utilized in Chilton County to eradicate the infestation of the Texas Fever Tick. *Glenn Littleton.*

appointed to supervise twenty-seven dipping vats being operated as part of the eradication program.

Adoption of the statewide law did not reduce tensions on the issue. A subsequent article in the *Union Banner* included the warning that "dynamiters have succeeded in demolishing nearly one-half of the dipping vats in Chilton

County." Vandalism became such a problem that Sheriff H.A. Harris was forced to deputize men to guard the vats during overnight hours.

Eventually, the practice of cattle dipping was grudgingly accepted throughout the county. In Clanton, cattle dipping even became a spectator sport. The *Union Banner* reported, "There was wholesale dipping of cattle at the new vat located on the hillside near the city water tank, with many interested spectators attending the event."

As 1918 came to a close, residents of Chilton County had two reasons to be thankful: the defeat of the Kaiser in Europe and the defeat of the miserable Texas Fever Tick at home. Once again, peace, harmony and goodwill abounded around the world and in Chilton County.

Bibliography

Armour, Mark, and Derek Norin. *The Great Eight: The 1975 Cincinnati Reds*. Lincoln, NE: University of Nebraska Press, 2014.

Blount, Roy, Jr. *Save Room for Pie: Food Songs and Chewy Ruminations*. New York: Sarah Crichton Books, 2016.

Blount, Russell W., Jr. *Wilson's Raid: The Final Blow to the Confederacy*. Charleston, SC: The History Press, 2018.

Bower, Emma Frank (chair, First Baptist Church of Clanton History Committee). *History of First Baptist Church, 1872–1983*. N.p., 1983.

Chilton County Heritage Book Committee. *The Heritage of Chilton County Alabama*. Clanton, AL: Heritage Publishing Consultants, 2000.

Chilton County (AL) News. Copies are available in the Genealogical Reference Room of the Chilton-Clanton Public Library.

Clanton Study Club. *A History of Chilton County*. Clanton, AL: Early Enterprises, 1927.

Clone, Wayne. *Alabama Railroads*. Tuscaloosa: University of Alabama Press, 1997.

Dennis, Blanche, and Lorene LeCroy. *Maplesville: The Town and the People: 1820–1989*. Montevallo, AL: Times Printing, 1989.

Hughes, Delos. *Historic Alabama Courthouses*. Montgomery, AL: New South Books, 2017.

Jackson, Harvey H., III. *Putting Loafing Streams to Work: The Building of Lay, Mitchell, Martin, and Jordan Dams, 1910–1929*. Tuscaloosa and London: University of Alabama Press, 1997.

———. *Rivers of History, Life on the Coosa, Tallapoosa, Cahaba and Alabama*. Tuscaloosa and London: University of Alabama Press, 1995.

Keister, Douglas. *Stories in Stone: A Field Guide to Cemetery Symbolism and Iconography*. Salt Lake City, UT: Gibbs Smith, 2004.

Lawson, Thomas. *Logging Railroads of Alabama*. Birmingham, AL: Cabbage Stack Publishing, 1996.

Parrish, Helen. "A History of the Clanton United Methodist Church" Unpublished manuscript, n.d. Clanton First United Methodist Church Library.

Racine, Kree Jack. *Above All: The Story of the Famous Blackwood Brothers Quartet*. Memphis, TN: Jarodoce Publications, 1967.

Shay, Jack. *The Fort McClellan POW Camp: German Prisoners in Alabama, 1943–1946*. Jefferson, NC: McFarland and Company, 2016.

Smith, Eugene A. *Geographical Survey of Alabama, Report of Progress for 1874*. Montgomery, AL: W.W. Screws, State Printer, 1875.

Truett, Mamie. "Baker County." Unpublished manuscript, 1938. Alabama Department of Archives and History Vertical File SG006834, Folder No. 005.

Wyatt, T.E. *Chilton County and Her People*. Montevallo, AL: Times Printing, 1976.

Wyeth, John. *The Life of Nathan Bedford Forrest*. New York: Harper and Brothers, 1899.

About the Author

Billy J. Singleton is the author of five books and has written extensively on the history of Chilton County and the state of Alabama. He earned a bachelor of science degree from Troy University and a master's degree in aerospace science from Embry-Riddle Aeronautical University. He has served as chair of the board of directors of the Alabama Aviation Hall of Fame and the Southern Museum of Flight, president of the Chilton County Chamber of Commerce and a member of the board of directors of the City of Clanton Arts Council. As a newspaper columnist, he has traveled the backroads of Chilton County to discover unique and unusual stories relating to the people, places and events hidden by the passage of time.